good
juju

About the Author

Najah Lightfoot is an initiated member of La Source Ancienne Ounfo, a private Vodou society in New Orleans, Louisiana, a sister-priestess of the Divine Feminine and an active member of the Denver Pagan community.

She keeps her magick strong through the practice of Kung Fu, the folk magick of Hoodoo, Pagan rituals, and her belief in the mysteries of the universe. She finds inspiration in movies, music, and the blue skies of Colorado. Najah is also a regular contributing author to the Llewellyn Almanac series. Her articles appear in Llewellyn's Witches' Datebook, Magical Almanac, Witches' Companion, and Spell-A-Day series.

To Write the Author

If you wish to contact the author or would like more information about this book, please write to the author in care of Llewellyn Worldwide, and we will forward your request. Both the author and publisher appreciate hearing from you and learning of your enjoyment of this book and how it has helped you. Llewellyn Worldwide cannot guarantee that every letter written to the author can be answered, but all will be forwarded. Please write to:

Najah Lightfoot
⁒ Llewellyn Worldwide
2143 Wooddale Drive
Woodbury, MN 55125.2989

Please enclose a self-addressed stamped envelope for reply,
or $1.00 to cover costs. If outside the USA, enclose
an international postal reply coupon.

good juju

mojos, rites
& practices
for the
magical soul

najah lightfoot

Llewellyn Publications
Woodbury, Minnesota

FIRST EDITION
Fourth Printing, 2021

Book design: Samantha Penn
Cover design: Ellen Lawson
Editing: Rosemary Wallner

Llewellyn Publications is a registered trademark of Llewellyn Worldwide Ltd.

Library of Congress Cataloging-in-Publication Data
Names: Lightfoot, Najah, author.
Title: Good juju : mojos, rites, and practices for the magical soul / Najah
    Lightfoot.
Description: First edition. | Woodbury, MN : Llewellyn Publications, 2019. |
    Includes bibliographical references.
Identifiers: LCCN 2019006101 (print) | LCCN 2019015966 (ebook) | ISBN
    9780738756677 (ebook) | ISBN 9780738756455 (alk. paper)
Subjects: LCSH: Magic.
Classification: LCC BF1611 (ebook) | LCC BF1611 .L473 2019 (print) | DDC
    133.4/3--dc23
LC record available at https://lccn.loc.gov/2019006101

Llewellyn Publications
A Division of Llewellyn Worldwide Ltd.
2143 Wooddale Drive
Woodbury, MN 55125.2989
www.llewellyn.com

Printed in the United States of America

This book is dedicated to my family. From my heart of hearts I thank my husband, Tim Bagley, and our wonderful son and daughter, Robert P. Herrmann and Kelly Bagley, for always standing by my side, loving me and supporting me, unconditionally.

contents

acknowledgments

This book would not have been possible without the support and encouragement of many people. I would like to thank Melanie Marquis, Elysia Gallo, John Kulsar, Kaewyn Picard, Sharon and David Soard, Andrea Neff, Rick F., Jennifer Dickey, Kara Seal, Leah Parker, Cynthia Richards, Judy Martindale, Laurie Martindale Goldberg, Colleen Ring, Taylor Schell, Cheryl Stratten, Arthur, Natalie Zaman, Melissa Susan Breton, Nancy Batty, Pamela McAlpin, Catherine Yronwode, Lou Florez, Gretchen and Richard Ashburn, Lois Harvey, Aameerah and Bob Swanson, Bette Smith-Milne, and Sallie Ann Glassman.

I humbly, fervently, and respectfully pay my respects to the divine Marie Laveau and Aunt Clara.

introduction

A woman stands on the seashore. Her smile is so bright, even the sun takes notice. She waves a smoldering bundle of herbs through the air, kisses the ground, and laughs. From her state of magical bliss, she looks into your eyes and says, "Good juju to YOU!"

What is good juju?

Good juju is the positive vibration of spirit. It is a dance with magick. It is time-honored traditions, rites, and practices that originated from African, North American, and European peoples.

It is the folk magick of the heart, the mojos of love, the rituals of earth, and the delight in the morning sun. It is blessings from the ancestors, goodness from the moon, and growth from trying new ways of doing things until they became as familiar to you as a comfortable pair of shoes. Good juju is a walk with nature, body, mind, and spirit. Good juju aids you in your quest to learn practical magick, which is available for you to use in your everyday life.

Good juju is a handshake with the world of spirit. It welcomes you as a divine magical being.

1

As the author of this magical book, it is my belief that many of us who are called to these paths are seekers. In my quest to merge spirituality with magical practices, I've walked many paths. Some paths took me to the tops of mountains, while others left me down in the valley. But no matter where I've been on the path of magical spirituality, I've discovered new things about myself, kept going, and held on to my childlike wonder of the mysteries.

Thus this book is born from my dreams, visions, and experiences. I am an initiated member of a private Vodou society in New Orleans, La Source Ancienne Ounfo, led by the dear, loving, powerful, and blessed Manbo Sallie Ann Glassman. I hold the rank of second-degree black belt, conferred upon me by my loving martial arts family, masters David and Sharon Soard, of the Chinese Shao-lin Center in Denver, Colorado. I am also a certified Lucky Mojo Practitioner, a title conferred upon me by my wonderful Hoodoo teacher, Catherine Yronwode of Lucky Mojo.com.

It is from these wonderful paths I come to you with my knowledge, skills, and abilities.

This book will help you lay the foundation for a daily ritual practice, tune into and listen to your intuition, and find ways to align with your Higher Power. We'll cover basic guidelines for working spells, tap into the powerful world of African-American folk magick, known as Hoodoo, and learn a ritual for prosperity and abundance.

As you journey through these divinely inspired spiritual traditions, you'll also learn how to craft mojos, create and work with altars, learn the benefits of protection magick, as well as how to maintain your individuality as a magical person. You'll also learn useful tips for keeping your mind, body, and spirit strong, through daily physical practices, which will help keep you grounded and centered.

As an added bonus, we'll also spend a moment on the Bayou St. John, honoring a headwashing ceremony, in the sacred religion of Vodou.

And although these topics are considered serious magical work, we'll end with some lighthearted anecdotes that will remind you we're all human, we all make mistakes, and even the best of us flub up from time to time. The lesson is to keep practicing and don't give up!

Many blessings and good juju to you, my magical friends!

—Najah Lightfoot

knock upon
the magical door

YOU'RE STANDING IN FRONT of bookshelves laden with every magical, mystical, and mysterious topic known to humankind. From a sunlit corner, sweet incense smoke spirals toward the ceiling. Crystals ranging in color from dark purple to pale lavender sparkle as light pours through a window in the framed-in turquoise shutters.

You've been here many times before. You've stood before this shelf wondering if you are a Witch, a Shaman, a Hoodoo mama, or a mojo daddy. Your only wish is to knock upon the magical door and step across the threshold, but you question if you're even at the *right* door, and furthermore if you do knock, who or what will respond?

Guess what? You have indeed knocked upon the right magical door, and I am here to welcome you, guide you, and assist you on your journey as a magical being.

We will walk together, you and I, as you try new ways of practicing magick, learn crafts and a bit of

5

Conjure, work spells, and grow into the powerful magical person you know you were meant to be. But steady on, my friend. Before we attempt to begin any of these rites and practices, we must start at the beginning... one ritual, one craft, and one spell at a time.

As we begin at the beginning, we start with good intentions to lay the foundation of our spiritual house. Your "house" is the metaphor for all the knowledge, skills, and tools you will acquire as you journey on your path as a magical, spiritual being.

Slowly over time, as you lay one magical brick of experience upon the other, your house will take shape. As you seek knowledge, skills, and experiences from the cupboards of life, you may find yourself gathering spiritual bricks from different masons. Some bricks may click right into place, some may need a bit of sanding to smooth out rough edges, and others may not fit regardless of how you try to arrange them.

A person can go nuts trying to fit all these different types of bricks into their spiritual house!

So before your load gets too heavy, stop for a moment and breathe. Learn to use your inner guidance, sense of discernment, and intuition by learning how to ground and center.

Ground and Center Yourself

As you journey along the magical path, it is crucial for your development as a magical and spiritual person to learn how to ground and center your being. Practicing magick can be quite a heady experience, especially when you are learning new rites, rituals, and practices. As you spread your wings and test new skills, it can be easy to feel lost and untethered, whether you're new to the magical path or a savvy practitioner.

All of us as magical people, whether we're old hats at magick or just beginning, need to be able to ground and center when we feel we're getting ahead of ourselves or when we're getting comfortable with magical practices unfamiliar to us.

▲▲▲▲▲▲▲▲▲▲▲▲▲▲▲▲▲▲▲▲▲▲▲▲
Rite for Grounding and Centering

This rite uses water, which cleanses, refreshes, and renews. Water washes away negativity and renews our bodies, minds, and spirits. Human beings can exist for several days without eating food but will perish quickly without drinking water. Water is life.

Items needed:
    A quiet place where you will not be disturbed
    Cool water
    A white taper or tealight candle and matches

Begin your grounding and centering rite by washing your face with cold water. Splash water upon your face, the back of your neck, your arms, and hands. As you bring water to your body, visualize a clear, cold stream running over rocks and meandering into deep green forests filled with tall trees and sunlit branches.

Once you have finished, pat yourself dry with a soft towel or cloth.

Gather your candle and go to your quiet place where you will not be disturbed. Sit comfortably in a position that allows both feet to be firmly planted on the floor, your back and neck in a straight upright position, and your hands placed either on your knees or on a table with the palms facing upward.

Light your candle.

Close your eyes.

Inhale naturally through your nose and exhale naturally through your mouth.

Don't force your breath. Just allow your breathing to come naturally.

When you feel ready, close your mouth, breathe naturally through your nose and open your eyes. Take a moment to allow your gaze to soften as you stare at the candle flame. Do you see any images? Notice the thoughts and visions that flow through your mind.

Close your eyes again. Gently inhale through your nose and exhale through your mouth as you allow any images or messages you have received to pass through your mind.

When you are naturally ready to end the exercise, open your eyes, pinch or snuff out the candle flame, rise, and go about your day.

▼ ▼ ▼ ▼ ▼ ▼

Repeat this exercise anytime you feel the need to ground and center. Pinching or snuffing out the candle flame allows the candle to be reused until the wick is almost burned out. When you sense the wick is getting low, use the candle to light another candle for your exercise. This way, you will form a continuous magical link from one candle to another, from one grounding and centering exercise to another. In time, you may find you are able to call forth the image of the candle to ground and center, which can be helpful if you are unable to be in your quiet place.

You may choose to add soothing music to the exercise. Meditative music calms the mind and soothes the soul. Sounds of the ocean, soft flutes, or piano melodies are a wonderful addition to this exercise.

Build a Solid Foundation

Now that you are armed with a practice for grounding and centering (which you can return to anytime you feel it is needed), you can take a leap of faith and challenge yourself to grow as a magical and spiritual person.

The rituals that follow will help you build a solid foundation for your magical, spiritual practice. They are designed to be used on a daily, monthly, or seasonal basis. Through time and effort, you will discover which frequency works best for you. Always remember this is your house. You are the builder and the architect. If something doesn't fit or work for you, it's okay to discard it and try something new.

Magical people work with the power of the mysteries, the ancestors, and ancient ways. Our goal is to bring the old ways into modern times. Although we may long for old temples, secret hallways, and lit torches, we must embrace the here and now. Sooty hallways and cobblestones may sound romantic and mystical, but I don't know too many people who would like to give up electricity or the internet! However, that doesn't mean from time to time we can't turn off the lights, disconnect from our phones, and light a candle to help us find our way.

To start building our spiritual house, we'll lay our foundation using spiritual rites and practices that, if used on a consistent basis, will become the mortar that holds your spiritual house together. Even though you decide to move the furniture around or paint your house a different color, the foundation always remains solid and must be cared for if you want your house to stand for years to come.

To begin building your spiritual foundation, start with a magical ritual that embraces the dawn of a new day and acknowledges the opportunities of a new beginning with each sunrise. Once you've said hello to the dawn, we'll move into a ritual many consider a cornerstone of magical practices: cleansing your space.

Next, we'll lay the final stone of our foundation with a practice for writing down your thoughts, feelings, and experiences, as it's good practice to keep notes on where you've been and where you're headed as you travel the magical pathways, guided by the sun, moon, and stars.

As you knock upon the magical door, may it swing wide open for you. May it welcome you and bestow upon you good juju, magical rites, rituals, and practices. May these rites and practices aid your magical soul as you navigate the twists and turns of magical, mystical spirituality.

Greet the Dawn

Sunrise brings the golden light of a new day. Dawn brings the promise of new beginnings, hope, and renewal.

Whatever happened yesterday is gone. It's in the past. You can't change it or revise it, no matter how much you may wish to change your decisions or actions. A new day beckons you to go forward.

If yesterday was a bad day, a new day brings you the opportunity to learn from your mistakes, take a breath, and carry on. If yesterday was a good day, a new day brings you the opportunity to bank on yesterday's blessings and move forward.

This ritual focuses on the power of prayer and the ritualistic power of beginning your day by calling the directions. The ritual described gives fuel to our thoughts and intentions. It is a tool to help us move forward in life, beginning with the light of a brand new day.

We all have morning routines. Some of us, like myself, blindly stumble to the coffeepot and don't truly awake until the Goddess of caffeine kisses our lips and awakens our senses with a hot cup of coffee.

Others don running clothes and head out for a morning jog. Some grab the dog and go for a first walk, taking in the sounds and smells of a new day.

Many may choose to head to the gym, yoga studio, or quiet place in their home to begin exercise routines.

All of these activities are valid and wonderful ways to start your day, but what about paying attention to your spirit and inner self?

Just as we awake to a new day, trying to get ourselves right and ready for what lies ahead, nature is doing the same thing. Birds are stretching their wings, getting ready to take flight. Squirrels and other critters are sniffing out their first meal. Leaves await the first light to begin their process of photosynthesis.

The first light brings so many opportunities to unite with spirit. If you're a night worker, use the ritual to set your dreamtime by entering into a state of peace before closing your eyes for sleep.

▲▲▲▲▲▲▲▲▲▲▲▲▲▲▲▲▲▲▲▲▲▲▲▲

Ritual of Calling the Directions

Many versions and rites exist for calling the directions. In its simplest form, it's a way of greeting the day and honoring the cardinal directions of east, south, west, and north. There are elaborate ways to perform this ritual and there are simple ways.

After many years of performing rites and rituals, I've found keeping things simple and direct to be the most powerful way to connect with your Higher Power. We are all busy people. Nothing sabotages a practice like feeling it won't fit with your schedule.

To begin this ritual, if you're able to be outside, get outside and benefit from being out in the morning air. Realistically, I know not all of us have backyards or are in places where we can easily get outside. Our dwelling may constrict us or weather may be a factor. However, I've found this ritual to be amenable to wherever you live or however the weather may be on a particular day. I have performed it many times from the comfort of my hotel room or in places where I couldn't get outside.

My version of this ritual focuses on seven directions: east, south, west, north, above, below, and within. Let's spend a few moments with each direction and some of their corresponding properties.

East

East is the direction of the element of air and a new beginning. It is the power of the rising sun, the rise of a new day. It is the power of our breath and the direction of our thoughts.

Breathe in the power of air. Let it fill you, lift you, take your mind and soul to a higher dimension.

South

South is the direction of the element of fire. It is the direction of our passions, flames of desire, and growth.

Breathe in the power of fire, heat, and warmth. Reflect upon warm climates, the spring and summer months, plants growing and leaves unfurling. Feel the flames of spirit rising and the heat from the spiritual fire that warms our soul.

West

West is the direction of the element of water, adventure, mountains, lakes and streams, and oceans. It is the direction of fall, of things accomplished, of going into one's inner self for reflection.

Breathe in the power of water. Reflect upon great bodies of water, such as the seas and oceans. Feel the coursing, powerful energy of rivers and streams.

North

North is the direction of the element of earth, the season of winter and all those who have gone before us.

Breathe in the scent of earth. Let the earth hold you and ground you. Remember all those who have gone before you. Bow and give them a nod of respect. Think upon the deep quiet of winter. Reflect upon the earth resting and healing. Let the direction of north empower and sustain you.

Above

The sky humbles us. It covers our days and blesses our nights. It is filled with the sun, moon, and stars. Beyond what we can see, galaxies, planets, black holes, gigantic suns, and universes exist, and we can only imagine them.

Breathe in the great beyond. Let it open you to the mysteries and magick of life.

Below

Stand firmly upon Mother Earth. Breathe in her willingness to provide us with everything we need, while knowing all things must return to lie in her body. Nothing exists which does not come from the earth. Know all creatures, humans, and creations of humankind will return to lie in the body of our Mother Earth.

Honor Mother Earth for her gifts of life and nourishment.

Within

Embrace the Divine within yourself. Feel the strength and power that rises from the soul of your being.

Visualize a pillar of light emanating from your core that connects you to the Divine Mysteries. Know you are loved, guided, and protected. Know you are a Divine Being incarnated in human form.

Performing the Ritual

Begin in the east, turning clockwise as you face each direction. Facing east, with arms spread wide, say,

> *Benedicite Dea. Benedicite Dea. Benedicite Dea!*
> [Latin for "Bless ye, Goddess!"] *Hail to the golden sun
> and this brand-new day of living, which has surely
> begun. Hail to the moon and stars so bright. Thank you,
> Goddess* [or Deity of your choice], *for your love,
> light, presence, and protection in my life. Hail and
> welcome powers of air, powers of east!*

Facing south, with arms spread wide, say,

> *Hail and welcome powers of fire,*
> *powers of south!*

Facing west, with arms spread wide, say,

> *Hail and welcome powers of water,*
> *powers of west.*

Facing north, with arms spread wide, say,

> *Hail and welcome powers of earth, powers of north.*
> *Blessed be all those who have gone before us.*

Facing east, with arms spread wide, look up to the sky and say,

> *Hail to the Queen of Heaven* [or your personal Deity]
> *that I love, the moon, stars, and planets above.*

Bend your knees, slowly lowering your hands to the ground and then raising them above your head. Visualize a tree growing upwards as you say,

> *Blessed be our sacred Mother Earth,*
> *without whom we would not be.*

Cross your hands over your heart. Say,

> *Blessed be the Divine Spirit, that I am,*
> *that is me, that are we.*

Stand with your arms spread wide and face the east. At this time, call out the names of people, places, things, and loved ones you would like to bless for the day.

End the ritual with the sign of the pentagram (see directions below) and by saying:

Blessed be, so mote it be.
▼ ▼ ▼ ▼ ▼ ▼

To make the sign of the pentagram:

Touch two fingers to your forehead.

Touch two fingers to your right breast.

Touch two fingers to your left shoulder.

Touch two fingers to your right shoulder.

Touch two fingers to your left breast.

Touch two fingers to your forehead.

As you continue to perform this ritual, it will grow and evolve to contain phrases, words, and motions that are personal to you, and that is a wonderful thing. The most powerful rituals are ones that have your unique and special touch to them. As you practice this ritual on a daily basis, making a sincere connection with the Divine, you will be guided toward words that have powerful and sacred meanings to you.

Feel free to revise this ritual and adapt it to suit your needs. It is written as a framework to help you lay your spiritual foundation. As you grow in strength, confidence, and power, it too will develop and expand.

Now go out and have yourself a wonderful day!

Cleanse Your Space—The Benefits of Smudging

Air represents the powers of the mind.

Our thoughts are directly tied to our emotions and our physical well-being. Our thoughts affect how we feel about others, ourselves, and our relationship to the world.

In the tarot, the suit of swords is attributed to the element of air. The swords symbolize cutting through the jumbles of the mind. They also represent negative emotions, which can ruin our day and sometimes even our lives.

There is the paralyzing card of the Three of Swords, the imagery of the stabbed heart, which needs little explanation. There's the frightening card of the Nine of Swords, displaying nightmares and terrors that steal your peace in the middle of the night.

I have experienced the terrifying depths of depression and anxiety. I've suffered through my own dark night of the soul.

I've been helped by the courage of friends and by professionals trained to help when more than just a casual conversation was needed.

I've taken antidepressants. I've been diagnosed as being clinically depressed after suffering a severe bout of postpartum depression twenty-seven years ago. I give much gratitude to those who helped me face my fears and heal my traumas.

As we work with the element of air, may we always remember we never need sail the rough seas alone. Help is always available. May there never be any shame in seeking professional help, especially when things become more than you can handle. There are many wonderful, loving, qualified people who commit their entire lives to helping us move forward and heal from life's trying times.

This ritual is written to provide spiritual support by working with the element of air, plants, herbs, and barks, which are said to uplift and heal the spirit through the action known as smudging. One can smudge themselves, their home, their office, or even sacred items on a daily basis.

Performing the rite of smudging is a wonderful way to bring calm, healing energy to your mind, body, and spirit, especially during times of stress. As magical people, we look to the element of air and the gifts Mother Nature provides to help us when times are tough. However, it must be stated to never substitute magick in place of seeking professional help when it is needed. One need not rule out the other. Both modalities can and do work famously together to bring healing, hope, and balance to one's life.

Smudging

Smudging is the act of purifying and cleansing. It is a sanctifying ritual to release negativity through the burning of incense or herbs. Smudging uses the power of air to clear negative feelings or emotions that you may feel are attached to a person, place, or thing. The ritual of smudging can be used as a gateway to prayer or as an act to bless yourself, talismans, crystals, or other magical items you may bring into your practice.

White sage is the most commonly used herb for smudging. Go to any metaphysical store or spiritual supply shop and you'll find lots of bundles of white sage, tied and ready to take home for use in your spiritual practices.

In my experience of burning white sage, when using it for spiritual purposes, the sage seems to know exactly how much smoke to release and how long to burn. Sometimes you'll get a lot of smoke. Sometimes you'll get very little.

There is also the question of how to put out a burning sage bundle. When I began burning sage bundles, I tried to put them out by sticking them in a pile of dirt. But I quickly learned sage bundles burn like an ember. They can remain hot and burn deeply from the core. So for my own peace of mind, I always put them out by sprinkling water over the burning bundle.

One sage bundle can last a long time, especially if you're lighting it for short periods of time on a daily basis. There are times when burning an entire sage bundle may be called for, such as in an outdoor ritual or when a deep home cleansing is needed. You could then allow the bundle to go out on its own. Just be sure you have plenty of windows open in your house and allow the bundle to burn in a fireproof container.

Although spiritual stores abound, if possible, try buying your sage from Native American people. In my hometown of Denver, Colorado, the Denver March Powwow comes to town in the last part of March, near or after the spring equinox. At the powwow, many vendors sell all types of wonderful items you just can't live without. I always stock up on my sage for the year at the powwow. You get better prices than you would in a store, and your money goes directly to supporting Native American people.

Palo Santo, Lavender, and Sweetgrass

You can find sage combined with cedar or lavender. There is also the wonderful dried and braided sweetgrass. Sweetgrass has a wonderful earthy, sweet scent. Its scent lingers in a room or space for long times without actually burning it. Sweetgrass doesn't actually burn or smoke as well as a white sage bundle. Perhaps this is why more people prefer using white sage bundles.

Many people also use Palo Santo. Palo Santo is a holy wood for smudging. I love its sweet woody smell. I've kept a stick of Palo Santo on my prosperity altar for many years. Just light the tip and allow the smoke to bless your space.

You can also smudge with incense. *Incense* is a catchall term that can refer to scented cones, hand-rolled sticks, or resins and powders that you burn on charcoal disks. Incense changes, affects, and lifts your mood. It takes you to different levels of spirit. It settles the heart and the mind.

Choose incense using your intuition. Browse the wonderful packets along with their mystical names. The possibilities are endless. Try burning different scents together. You may hit upon your own magical combination. As you work your way through the plethora of incense available, you may find companies or persons who make incenses that align with your spirit. That's a good thing. As you shop for incense, take time to view the different types of packaging. Some incenses come in tiny boxes. Some are wrapped in elaborate paper. Some are packaged with suns, moons, or mystical symbols incorporated into the packaging. Take notice of these features; someday, if you're a crafty person, you may create your own line of specialized incense.

Use common sense in your ritual work. Don't leave things burning unattended. If you're burning candles and working lengthy rituals, make sure your candles are in fireproof containers.

Incense, herbs, oils, and the ritual of smudging all take us through the power of air. Through smoke and scent, we release negativity, call in blessings, and open the door to prayers sent and received.

▲▲▲▲▲▲▲▲▲▲▲▲▲▲▲▲▲▲▲▲▲▲▲▲

Rite of Smudging

Items needed:

A lighter or matches

Appropriate smudge plant or woody bark such as white sage,
sweetgrass, or Palo Santo

OR

Loose incense of your choice

Charcoal disks (easily available at brick and mortar or online
metaphysical shops and sites), if you choose to burn loose
incense as your smudge material

Fireproof container to hold your burning charcoal disk

OR

A stick of your favorite incense

Depending upon the plant, herb, or incense you have chosen to use for smudging, light the material. If you have chosen a
white sage bundle, a braid of sweetgrass, a woody piece of Palo
Santo, or a stick of incense, light the tip using your lighter or
match. As the end of the material catches flame, gently waft the
herb or bark through the air until the flame goes out and only
smoke remains.

If you have chosen to use loose incense as your smudging material, light the edge of the charcoal disk and place the disk in the
fireproof container. The charcoal disk will spark and light quickly.
Allow the charcoal to burn until sparks can no longer be seen.
Once the sparks have gone out, your charcoal disk is now hot
(don't touch it with your hands) and ready to receive your loose
incense.

How to Smudge

Take a moment to ground and center.

Light your smudge material.

Say this smudging prayer:

> *I give thanks for this* [insert the name of
> your smudging material, i.e., white sage,
> Palo Santo, sweetgrass, or incense]. *I give thanks
> for the healing, calming, cleansing energy it brings
> to my life and to my days and nights.
> As above, so below; this healing
> energy is with me wherever I go.
> With the power of this smoke,
> blessed energy do I invoke.
> By the power of three times three,
> sacred, loving energy is always with me.*

If you are smudging yourself, use your hand to wave the smudge smoke over your body.

If you are smudging an object, pass the object through the smudge smoke.

If you are smudging a space, such as your home or office, walk through the space with the smoking smudge and a fireproof container to catch falling ashes, wafting the smoke through the air as you walk from room to room.

When you are finished smudging, safely put out the smoking material by either passing it through water (so you are sure the smudge bundle is out) or placing a lid atop your fireproof container.

▼ ▼ ▼ ▼ ▼ ▼

Write It Down—The Benefits of Journaling

It's funny. The day I began writing this chapter, I found myself without a journal. I usually have a journal waiting in the wings, so when one journal ends, I can begin a new one without interruption. But that is not the case today. Today, I will need to shop for a new journal, which is a spiritual task I enjoy doing.

I love looking at new journals, holding them, feeling the weight of their paper. I like seeing how they're bound, studying their cover art or lack thereof, reading where they were printed or how they were printed. To me, a journal is a living being. Its essence is born from the trees from which it was made, the bindings, and its creator's intention.

A journal holds your secrets, your wishes, your dreams and desires. It is your friend: your ally in dark times, and your cheerleader in good times.

In today's technological world, many of our thoughts are transcribed on digital devices, but for the sake of this spiritual tool, I encourage you to get a physically printed and bound journal. There is a dynamic that happens when mind, pen, and paper begin a relationship. It's a magical experience. And if you're a scribe, the relationship between your thoughts and paper is a cherished one.

I've often felt I would write on walls if I had no paper. Perhaps that's what makes me a writer, the overwhelming need to express myself literally.

As children we discover journaling in the form of diaries, this being especially true for little girls. Boys tend to have notebooks where they can keep their secret thoughts and feelings. Girls tend toward journals or diaries that have locks, keys, whimsical whatnots, and hidden compartments.

As adults in the magical realm, some of our journals have dual lives as Books of Shadows, where we store and log our magical journeys. A journal can be set up any way you like it. It should be a friend you go to when you feel called to reflect and ponder. It's not a chore or a "have to"; it's a place of serenity and introspection.

Many years ago, I completed Julia Cameron's *The Artist's Way,* in which she suggests writing morning pages. Since I was already a journaler, this was an easy task for me, but if journaling isn't your thing, I can see how this would be a daunting task. Yet even as a journaler and one who has journaling practice, I too benefited from making my journaling a priority every morning for a specific amount of days. It is good to write things down.

Sometimes when you think of journaling you may worry about someone finding your words, reading your deepest thoughts without your permission. Personally, I consider reading someone's journal without permission an act of treason, a moral infraction of the highest caliber. A person's journal is a place for their soul feelings and should always be respected as such. Never read someone's journal (or go snooping through their things) without the owner's permission. One should be allowed to have privacy in their own home or dwelling without the fear of others trespassing.

If the above is not the case for you, if you feel you can't write and keep your words private, find a place to write where you can maintain your privacy. Since you will be writing on paper, you can always burn your pages when you're finished. That way, you can be sure no one will ever read what you have written down.

Journaling as a Spiritual Practice

Journaling clears the mind. The more you write, the better you feel. If you can turn off your inner critic and allow your words to flow, you will embark upon a journey of self-discovery unlike any other. In addition, if you keep your journals, you will have a living history of where you have been, your failures and accomplishments, and how you overcame life's challenges. If you are truly inspired by your words, you may bequeath your journals to a loved one or an organization to receive upon your passing. Just think of the enormous perspective you can have on someone who reads your journal a hundred years from now. You'd be giving them a bird's-eye view into what life was like during your sojourn on earth.

Journals come in all shapes and sizes, from tiny pocket and purse sizes to enormous tomes of paper. They can be moleskin notebooks or handcrafted creations. Creating a journal can be a fun and easy craft. The covers can be as simple as using construction paper with blank paper, either stapled, glued, or bound together with yarn. You can decorate their covers or inner pages however you choose.

A journal is a blank canvas for your thoughts. Journaling is not meant to be a stressful task; it is intended to be the direct opposite. It is a practice to help you release tension and stress, and help you find ways and paths in your spiritual journey you may not have considered.

Some people may balk at the terror of staring at a blank page. Writers have that fear all that time! But you are not writing a book for public view. It's for your eyes only, so you can begin however you wish. Below are a few suggestions that may help to get you started.

Make it a priority to have a quiet place to journal. This doesn't always have to be your home. You can journal anywhere; parks, bookstores, libraries, and coffee shops all have places where you can find quiet corners to tuck into and write.

Invest in a good pen. By "good" I mean one that calls to you to use it. Pens can be very expensive, but it needn't be for the sake of journaling. Just make sure the pen feels good in your hands and that the ink flows well. There's nothing worse than sitting down to journal and finding your pen skips or is out of ink.

If writing words is hard for you, use your journal as a mini vision board. Place pictures, photos, souvenirs, pressed flowers, torn pages from magazines, fortune cookie notes, or anything else you like on the pages. You may find pasting or drawing an image on your pages will spur you into writing something. Have fun with the process.

There is no wrong or right way to journal. You can write as little or as much as you like. You can write in the morning, afternoon, or evening. You can journal on your break at work or when you wake up first thing in the morning. The possibilities are endless. This is your journal journey. Take it one page at a time.

▲ ▲
A Journal Spell

Below is a spell to help you get your journaling started.

Items needed:
   A candle and matches
   A journal and something to write with

Find a quiet place. Light a candle, if you so desire.

Hold your journal in your hands and close your eyes.

Feel the journal's spine, cover, and pages. Breathe in the scent of the paper. Visualize your journal filled with your thoughts.

Take a deep breath. Exhale and breathe over your journal.

Now write in your journal the first words that pop into your mind.

Close your journal and be with your power to create.

Blessed be.

▼ ▼ ▼ ▼ ▼ ▼

step through the magical curtain

WE'VE KNOCKED UPON THE magical door by greeting the dawn, cleansing our spaces, and learning the benefits of journaling. I hope you've been able to make a few notes in your journal that will help you monitor your progress on your path as a magical soul. And now as the curtain of your subconscious parts, your mind gives way to visions and images you may not have encountered before.

You may find yourself thinking about mystical adventures or journeys, which could take you to faraway places. You may have the need to start changing your wardrobe by adding flowing garments and magical talismans. An idea for a tattoo may begin to circulate in your thoughts, or you may find you have the overwhelming feeling to tear off your clothes and sit naked under the moonlight.

These thoughts and feelings are good and okay. They are your soul recognizing you've stepped into the mystical and mysterious. In the chapters that follow, we will

29

explore ways to build confidence using your intuition, learn a ritual for cleansing and protection that you can use anytime, and discuss some ways for working with your Higher Power, however that power shows up for you.

Although many of us are called to the magical curtain, hundreds, even thousands, never go through it. Some may be beholden to vows they took lifetimes ago and haven't yet let those vows go. Some may have the fear of ridicule or condemnation, which keeps them from pursuing paths mainstream society has not quite embraced.

And some may have the fear of themselves, terrified of what they may discover or find once they do step through the curtain. For deep within the psyche of many of us who are called to these paths are remembrances of times when people were persecuted for having beliefs and practices deemed unholy or demonic by others.

Delve into the historical records of time and you will find many examples of people harmed for practicing beliefs or faiths that mainstream society did not accept. History reveals a plethora of disturbing accounts of women and men persecuted for being Witches, such as the Salem Witch Trials in the United States, or of temples being razed for holding knowledge deemed heretical by conquering armies that were relentless in their pursuit to become the reigning power in a region. The destruction and the great loss of the library at Alexandria, for one example, still causes many a soul to wince.

It has also been said, "The Gods of the old become the demons of the new," and "History is written by the winners, not the losers."

Even today, people face persecution and ridicule for living their life as who they are, being who they were created to be. The fight for civil rights is still an ongoing and perpetual quest for dignity, recognition, and acceptance. The news is riddled with accounts by people in the LGBTQ community fighting for their human rights, African-Americans still fighting for civil rights, women marching and protesting against patriarchal and sexual harassment in the workplace, and immigrants fighting to be treated humanely. Sadly, as much as the world has changed, much still remains the same.

Embrace the Magick

But before these examples of persecution cause you not to proceed any further, remember your journey is a sacred walk, one many spiritual people before you have taken. Many have taken vision quests or gone on spiritual journeys to get in touch with their inner guides and Higher Powers. Studying occult knowledge or practicing folk magick does not make you a bad person! It doesn't take much to imagine oneself in ancient times seeking the counsel of an oracle, sitting with a medicine man as he prescribes an herbal remedy for your needs, looking for answers in tea leaves, or throwing bones to reveal answers to questions.

For to this day, many people seek the counsel of their Shaman, healer, or priest for assistance with the trials of life. Many people all over the planet light candles, observe traditions that honor the seasons, and have superstitions such as not cutting their hair until a goal is obtained or wearing the same clothes again and again until they reach a destination. Lots of people throw salt over their shoulders for good luck, or absolutely will not allow their foot to hang over the side of the bed when they sleep, for fear of sleep monsters carting them off in the middle of the night.

And in the tradition of Hoodoo and Conjure, many people seek the counsel of their rootworker, doctor, or auntie to help them navigate the waters of love, prosperity, success, and protection.

In addition to these avenues for connecting with spiritual power, words commonly associated with occult or magical practices have begun to show up in our daily language. The word *mojo* is commonly used. So are the words *Goddess, aromatherapy, voodoo, spell, vision, visualize, meditate,* and *Conjure.* It is not uncommon now for everyday people to take off to tropical islands or mountainous retreats seeking communion with Divine Beings or plant medicine to reveal the inner workings of the cosmos. Similarly, in the 1960s people liberally availed themselves of psychotropic drugs and psychedelic experiences, magically opening themselves to "tune out and tune in." And in 1997 the character of Harry Potter brought the world of magick to millions, endearing himself and his magical buddies to hearts and minds of young and old alike.

And on a mass scale, Halloween is now one of the most popular holidays in the United States. During the months leading up to October, catalogs and commercials arrive laden with advertisements for Witch's hats, pointy shoes, striped stockings, ghosts that fly from trees, and spooky solar lights made to make any home a place for fun and trickery. Add to that the invention of social media along with hashtags such as #witchesofinstagram, #goddess, #mystic and #earthmagick garner thousands of posts. It does indeed seem the time is right for practicing the old ways as we live in these modern times.

Embrace the call you have received from the Divine Mysteries of the universe. As the magical curtain parts for you, you will discover ways and skills to assist you on your journey of magick and spirituality. Through the pages of this book, we shall journey well, one magical rite and ritual at a time.

Listen to Your Intuition

You've been thinking about a person and suddenly, seemingly out of nowhere, you receive a text or a phone call from this person.

You're watching a TV show and you see the exact location you've been thinking about going to for a vacation.

You're in a crystal store and feel driven to pick up a certain stone. Upon reading the metaphysical properties about the stone, you realize it meets your exact needs, or thoughts, which have been flowing through your mind.

Are these examples of synchronicity? Are they magick? Are they serendipitous moments constructed by the higher forces of the universe just for you? I say yes. I say it's all of this and much more.

When you begin to focus your thoughts, will, and intentions on manifesting your goals, dreams, and desires, magical, synchronistic, and serendipitous things will begin to show up in your life.

But before these mysterious manifestations can appear, one must begin to build a magical environment for these special moments to gain a foothold and sprout their magical buds. One must prepare the fertile soil of their mind, much like tending to a garden before you decide to plant in it.

For our minds are like the soil of a garden. Left untended, all sorts of weeds and unsavory characters will take root. Some may even bind themselves to healthy thoughts and slowly choke them out, establishing their need to control and dominate. The garden of the mind—left untended—will grow weeds and attract mental pests. Pests and weeds, which can take hold and thrive, if care isn't given to keep the mind healthy on a daily basis.

First Things First

When you first begin to step into the magical world, you may want to purchase every book on the subject of metaphysics or the occult. You may be tempted to spend your last dollar on a talisman, crystal, or charm that promises to open a magical doorway or attend classes and get divination readings.

While all the above are valid ways to build a relationship with your intuition, your first and best guide will always be to follow your inner guidance and build confidence working with discernment.

Many a fellow traveler has fallen down the rabbit hole because they didn't pay attention to the nudges their inner guidance was giving them. When people first step onto the path of magick, many are swayed by colorful robes and fantastical promises. We're newbies, open, ready and willing. However, we do come to the table with our gifts, even if they haven't grown legs yet sturdy enough to stand on.

I believe it is safe to assume you are already a person familiar with signs and nudges, hunches and gut feelings, because you are reading a book about mojos, rites, and magical practices. You're ready to stand and walk through the door of working with your intuition on a higher level.

As with all good things, developing the power of your intuition takes time and effort. One of the best and often underutilized areas for connecting with our inner guidance is our dreams.

Working with Dreams

Some say the dream world is the real world. Some say the waking world is where we reside as earthly beings until we can return to the dream world where we are not bound by our human bodies and needs, and the parameters of the earthly plane. Some people are lucid dreamers, meaning they can consciously take control of their dreams while sleeping and make choices as to where their dream body takes them and what they do or experience in their dreams. When you can take control of your dreams and consciously make decisions while sleeping, you have indeed bridged the power of intuition, conscious thought, and self-will. Becoming a lucid dreamer takes time, effort, and practice. One of the best ways to start is to build your intuitive strength.

One tool for enhancing your intuition through the power of dreams is using the power of color. If you dream in color and find one color to be predominant, upon waking wear that color in some form. Wear your dream color as the color of your socks, your shirt or blouse, a barrette in your hair, or even as the color of your underwear, which no one can see but you. Knowing you are wearing your dream color can be a powerful magical stimulant to your mind and imagination.

When you bring your dream color into the waking world, you build a bridge between your subconscious and conscious mind. Your dream color may become a magical gatekeeper or talisman, one that opens the door to your dream world and intuitive powers as you continue to work with it.

As your dream color becomes prominent in your life, make it a permanent part of your wardrobe. It may become the color of your favorite shirt, tie, lipstick, blouse, shoes, or perhaps even your car!

Keeping a dream journal is also a wonderful way to work with the power of dreams. When selecting a dream journal, choose one with a cover image you find pleasing. Keep the journal and a pen or pencil next to your bed. When you awake from a dream, immediately write down all you remember.

In my experience of keeping a dream journal, I have found it quite difficult to reread my own handwriting after writing my thoughts in my dream journal. One does not have the best handwriting at two, three, or five o'clock in the morning! However, the act of writing down your thoughts immediately after dreaming is a good exercise for building a connection between your dream and waking world. And if you can read your handwriting, you may find messages or insights hidden within your dream transcripts.

Magical people are extremely drawn to imagery from the animal kingdom, plant kingdom, and nature. Many times these images appear in our dreams. As these symbols appear over and over again, they can become talismans or links to our intuition and subconscious minds. Many beginners use dream interpretation books to help decipher dream symbols. One of my all-time favorite books is *The Dream Book* by Betty Bethards, which contains more than fifteen hundred dream symbols. Over time, as certain images or symbols repeat in your dreams, you will develop a personal relationship with these symbols when you see them in your waking life. Using these symbols along with your intuition can be a valuable tool for building strength and skill as a magical person.

For example, butterflies may appear to you in your dreams. A butterfly could be a symbol of transformation (as a butterfly changes completely from one being to another as it emerges from its cocoon). If you are under stress or going through significant change in your life and butterflies appear in your dreams, it could be a sign that great and wonderful changes are about to appear in your life. Similarly, in your waking life if you are contemplating changes and a butterfly flies past, your intuitive self may take notice and interpret the butterfly as confirmation that great and wondrous changes are afoot!

Changing Things Up and Tools of Divination

Another tool for developing your intuition is to take a different route home or to a familiar destination. Allow your mode of transportation to be the instrument of your intuition. Perhaps where you always turn right, you turn left. Maybe you take the long way home instead of the short route. As you allow your intuition to guide you, pay close attention to the street signs and buildings. A never-before-seen billboard or signpost may be a message waiting just for you.

Another tool for stimulating your intuition is the art of bibliomancy, which is the art of using books for divination. To perform bibliomancy, sit quietly and comfortably. Grab a book. Close your eyes and allow your mind to focus on a question. While your eyes are closed, open the book and use your finger as a pointer. When you feel ready, stop scrolling with your finger. Open your eyes. The word or sentence on the page your finger is pointing to is the answer to your question.

You can also do the same exercise with tarot cards or runes. If you use cards or runes, I find that pulling a single card or choosing one rune is best when you're beginning. Close your eyes, focus on your question, and pull a single rune or tarot card. Take time to meditate on the meanings and feelings you get from your pull. Write a journal entry to record your feelings, thoughts, and observations.

As you explore and develop using your intuition as a guide, your confidence will grow. And if you still find yourself falling down a rabbit hole from time to time while developing your inner guidance, don't beat yourself up about it. The lesson is to learn from your journey and keep moving forward. The next road sign or path may be just the one you've been waiting for! Keep your intuitive eyes peeled and your heart open. Unless you are willing and ready to receive, you may never know what messages the universe is sending to you.

Call Upon the Archangels

The tracings and beginnings of the Lesser Banishing Ritual of the Pentagram (LBRP) can be found in the Kabbalah, the history of the Golden Dawn, and many other magical, mystical resources. One can drop into a serious rabbit hole, trying to understand and contemplate the origins of this mysterious and powerful ritual.

I make no claims in being a scholar of the Kabbalah, or in the practices of the Golden Dawn. However, the LBRP, as it is commonly known, was one of the first things I learned as a novice Witch. It is a simple ritual, yet one that takes a lifetime to master and maybe even longer to understand. It is the underlying occult principle in many practices and traditions. Even as I write these words, I continue to seek knowledge and wisdom about the LBRP. As magical persons, we should endeavor to continue to grow in knowledge, skills, and abilities.

Some use the LBRP before casting a circle as it clears negativity and calls upon the archangels and elements as protectors. Some use it on a daily basis to connect with the Divine and protect themselves. The LBRP is a practice, which evolves as you find comfort in using it.

The Lesser Banishing Ritual of the Pentagram includes Hebrew words and names of angels. It may or may not sit comfortably with you to use Hebrew or angelic names. In my practice of the LBRP, I have come to associate the names of angels with Higher Beings who help us in our journey as human beings. The Greek word *angelos* simply means *messenger*. At some level, we have subscribed to a belief in the unseen and its power, or we wouldn't be doing these practices or seeking to gain knowledge of occult rituals.

I find it not unreasonable that human kind would attribute names, titles, and actions to other worldly beings, which they call upon in times of comfort and stress. It is humbling to believe in a power greater than one's self. If you dig deep enough and do enough cross-referencing and research, you will find similar names and attributes to Higher Beings, which cross over many religions and faiths.

▲▲▲▲▲▲▲▲▲▲▲▲▲▲▲▲▲▲▲▲▲▲▲▲▲

The Lesser Banishing Ritual of the Pentagram

As with all rituals, ground and center yourself before you begin. Reflect upon the symbol of the pentagram, which is an ancient symbol of protection. The pentagram represents matter within the circle of life. Its five points represent earth, air, fire, water, and spirit, all contained within the never-ending cycle of life. Think upon the Vitruvian man or the energy of a magnificent star blazing brightly within the galactic circle of the universe. You may also find the image of the Magician in the tarot coming to you. You are creator and manifestor of your universe.

My description of the LBRP is a simple one. It is one I use as a daily practice. As you embrace and use the LBRP, you may find the need to change how you do it, use it, or say it. Changing and morphing rituals into ones that personally speak to you is the first sign of a true practitioner. Our Craft grows through creation, change, and practice.

To begin the LBRP, face east, feet firmly planted on the ground. Look up to the sky. Enter into a state of reverence.

Say,

> *With love, honor, grace, and humility,*
> *I call upon Thee.*

Raise the first two fingers on your right hand and say,

> *Ah-teh.*

Feel the power as you say,

> *I call forth.*

Look downward; point your two fingers toward the ground and say,

> *Mal-Kuth.*

Feel the power as you say,

> *I manifest.*

Touch your two fingers to your left shoulder and say,

Ve-Ge-Vu-Rah.

Touch your two fingers to your right shoulder and say,

Ve-Ge-Du-Lah.

Make two fists, cross your arms in front of your chest, and say,

Lih-oh-lahm-ameen.

Use the index and middle finger on your right hand to trace a banishing pentagram in the air. A banishing pentagram is a five-pointed star that begins by drawing the star upwards from the left point and enclosing the star in a circle.

Once you've drawn the banishing pentagram in the air, step forward, thrust your hands into the center, and say,

Yod-hay-vow-hay.

Draw a line in the air with your two fingers, as you turn to the south direction. Make another banishing pentagram. Thrust your hands through the center and say,

Ah-don-nai.

Draw a line in the air with your two fingers as you turn to the west direction. Make another banishing pentagram. Thrust your hands through the center and say,

Eh-hay-yay.

Draw a line in the air with your two fingers as you turn to the north direction. Make another banishing pentagram. Thrust your hands through the center and say,

Aug-lah.

Draw a final line in the air with your two fingers as you return to the east direction.

Facing east, stand with your feet spread lightly apart, back straight, arms outstretched (think upon the symbol of the Vitruvian man). You are now a five-pointed star.

Say,

Before me Raphael [Rah-fay-el].

Visualize the archangel Raphael in flowing yellow robes. Feel the power of the element of air.
Say,

Behind me Gabriel [Gahb-ray-el].

Visualize the archangel Gabriel in flowing blue robes. Feel the power of the element of water.
Say,

At my right hand Michael [Meek-ay-ael].

Visualize the archangel Michael in flowing red robes. Feel the power of the element of fire.
Say,

At my left hand Auriel [Ohr-ree-el].

Visualize the archangel Auriel in flowing brown robes.
Feel the power of the element of earth.
Say,

> For about me flame the pentagrams and
> within me shines the six-rayed star!

Visualize yourself surrounded by blue flaming pentagrams and a six-rayed star burning brightly inside you.

Close the ritual as you began:

Raise the first two fingers on your right hand, look to the sky, and say,

> Ah-teh.

Look downward, point your two fingers toward the ground, and say,

> Mal-Kuth.

Touch your two fingers to your left shoulder and say,

> Ve-Ge-Vu-Rah.

Touch your two fingers to your right shoulder and say,

> Ve-Ge-Du-Lah.

Make two fists, cross your arms in front of your chest, and say,

> Lih-oh-lahm-ameen.

Say a closing prayer of thanks to the archangels, guides, and Elementals for their constant blessings and eternal protection.

▼ ▼ ▼ ▼ ▼ ▼

As you become more comfortable with the Lesser Banishing Ritual of the Pentagram, consider adding a burning sage bundle as a wand, if you are able to perform the ritual outside. The smoke from the burning sage bundle adds depth to your ritual. Allow yourself to experience the magick as the smoke carries your words and prayers to the ethers of the spirit world.

The LBRP is a powerful occult ritual for cleansing, blessing, manifesting, and protection. I highly recommend further study of its history and power. Many books abound about the subject. I recommend practicing the ritual first and getting comfortable with the words. When you can do the ritual from memory, seek more information on its properties, history, and practices. In the reference section are several titles to help you expand your knowledge and practice of this powerful ritual.

Working with Your Higher Power

The spirit calls us in many ways. We are earth-based people, people who find inspiration, bliss, and blessings in the simple ways of nature. A bird may fly past you and suddenly you too are on the wings of spirit, floating through the sky, sailing into higher dimensions. A chime rings in a summer breeze and you find your mind's eye, gazing into thoughts of past lives in sacred temples. Staring at clouds in an azure sky opens your being to peace and serenity.

From these simple and divine ways comes the desire to connect with the Higher Powers of the universe. In our world, a

Higher Power can have many names, including Deity, Goddess, God, Father Sky, Mother Earth, Creator, Lwa, Orisha, and angel. All these names are human attempts to describe the unknowable and the unfathomable, that which simultaneously exists deep within ourselves and outside ourselves at the same time.

We reach for a connection with our Higher Power through acts of magick. We may find that connection through incense burning in a cauldron or candles lit on an altar. We may hold our hands open in prayer and supplication, or dance around the circle as drum beats drive us to an ecstatic state of bliss. We write petition papers to spirit to assist us in our needs. We honor the seasons as sacred, as we follow the turn of the Wheel, from winter to spring, spring to summer, summer to fall, and finally fall back to winter.

We connect with the Divine through honoring the full moons, thirteen times a year, or by lighting a simple candle as a daily practice. Each of these acts brings us closer and closer to developing an ongoing relationship with our Higher Power.

Forging a New Path

Many of us come to the worlds of Witchcraft, Hoodoo, Wicca, the sacred religion of Vodou, or the practice of folk magick from upbringings in organized religions. It can be hard to turn one's back on family traditions or faiths we've practiced for years yet have ceased to work for us. Be that as it may, years of training do not simply vanish in a puff of smoke. It can take decades to become comfortable with a new way. Many a seeker has had their doubts about walking a new and different path, which is completely valid and understandable.

When you feel called to work with a Higher Power of the Divine Mysteries, it is totally okay to question and have doubts. You may take two steps forward, then five steps back as you seek to form a relationship with this new expression of the Divine that calls to you. As you build this relationship, there is also no need to "throw the baby out with the bathwater." That is, sometimes we can move too fast in our quest to become initiated or dedicated in the worlds of the occult, the Divine, and the mysterious. It would do well to remember that these practices have been around since the beginning of time, and there is no need to rush. Celebrate and enjoy the journey!

As you do move forward, here are some simple steps you can take to build your relationship with your Higher Power (as it calls to you):

- **Set up a small shrine or altar.** Add a small statue, flowers or perfume in pretty bottles to attract the benevolence of the spirit.

- **Do research to learn if the Deity is associated with plants or herbs.** If so, consider planting flowers, plants, or herbs aligned with your Higher Power. Decorate a clay pot with symbols associated with your spirit guide. Glue quartz crystals on the pot for good vibrations, add some potting soil along with the plant or herb, thereby creating a living testament to your Higher Power. If you decided to plant herbs, use your spiritual herbs in your culinary adventures!

    Many Gods and Goddesses are also associated with specific flowers, foods, or drink. Add the favorite food or drink to the altar. Once the essence of the offering has been received, bury the remnants deep in the ground in your backyard, or throw the leftover food in running water, or simply pour the libation on the ground. Say thank you to the spirit and to the earth once you are finished disposing of the remnants. Returning the remnants of the offering to the earth, keeps the circle of connection between you, Mother Earth, and your Deity intact.

- **Research what may be important to the spirit.** Learn some of their favorite prayers or chants. Add a prayer or song to your Higher Power in your daily ritual.

- **Learn about significant rituals or rites ascribed to your Deity.** As you feel comfortable, slowly incorporate these practices into your life. For instance, a day of the week may be special to your Deity. Fridays are considered good days for love work as they are associated with the planet Venus. If you are working with the Goddesses of love, make an offering of love to your Goddess on that day.

  The colors blue and white are sacred to the Orisha Yemaya and to the Lwa Marie Laveau. Consider adding blue and white flowers, or sea salts and salted water to your altar if you are working with these benevolent beings of African traditions.

- **Make a pilgrimage to sites important to your Higher Power, Deity, spirit, or guide** (if your wallet can bear it). You may receive guidance or inspiration when you are physically in places considered sacred to your Higher Power. Spending time at a sacred site is also a wonderful way to pay your respects and get in touch with them on a more personal basis.

  As a personal example, I began to forge my relationship with the divine Marie Laveau after many years of traveling to New Orleans, visiting her tomb in St. Louis Cemetery No. 1, leaving offerings to her, and practicing Hoodoo. As I continued to work with Marie Laveau as a spiritual guide, I found myself slowly being brought into a deeper relationship with her.

Building Trust

Trust is important. It is important to keep an open mind and also keep your wits about you as you travel the roads of the Divine Mysteries. As you awake to guidance, nudges, hints, and intuitive pokes, be sure to check in with your gut feelings. Do you feel good when you perform new rituals that align with your Deity? Are you having good dreams about your chosen path? If your path has a community outlet, do you feel welcome when you attend events? Can you practice your walk without breaking your wallet? Sometimes people can go through many a dollar without ever receiving a penny's worth of true guidance and inspiration. And finally, can you be yourself as you grow and learn, or do you feel pressured to conform within the community?

These are all check-ins, to keep you grounded and your eyes open as a traveler on the mystical road. Always know you have the option to let go, quit, change your mind, or simply put things aside if you discover you are not getting what you need as you build a relationship with your Higher Power and/or new community.

One of the best things about being a magical and spiritual person is that we are free to shape our world as we see fit. We are free to experiment, incorporating what works for us and letting go of what doesn't.

▲ ▲▲ ▲

Self-Blessing Ritual

As you build trust and a relationship with your Higher Power and spiritual path, you may find yourself naturally drawn to the desire to become dedicated or formally initiated.

Many initiations require memberships or a formal welcoming into a community. Prior to reaching that level of spiritual commitment, however, one is more than welcome to self-bless or self-initiate themselves in a manner that is private and sincere to their path.

A self-blessing or dedication is a private ceremony, held between you, your Deity, and the walk of your spiritual path. You need not share this information with anyone. In fact, the ritual can be more powerful if kept to one's self, or written down in your magical journal.

Below are suggestions for a self-blessing ritual. Listen to your intuition, follow your heart, and approach the ritual with honest intentions and sincerity. What you do with honor and integrity will surely return manyfold blessings to you.

Items needed:
    Salt
    Fresh flowers
    A bowl of water
    Your favorite brand of stick incense
    Rose essential oil or rose-scented perfume
    Matches or a lighter

Arise early in the morning, before sunrise. Bathe yourself and put on fresh clothes. Gather the items together. Speak to no one, and, if possible, go outside.

Face the direction of east. Pick up the salt and say,

Blessed be element of salt.

Pick up the bowl of water and say,

Blessed be element of water.

Drop three pinches of salt into the water. Swirl the water around in the bowl, to mix the salt and the water.

Say,

Blessed be this salted water, which cleanses,
renews, protects, and refreshes.

Sprinkle some of the water on your head and on the ground around you.

Pick up the lighter and incense and say,

Blessed be element of fire. Blessed be this sacred smoke,
which carries my prayers I now invoke.

Light the incense stick. Wave the incense stick back and forth through the air until the flame goes out, and the incense stick begins to smoke.

Say,

> *With this smoke and with this fire, I channel*
> *blessings from my Higher Power.*

Swirl the wand of smoking incense around you. When done, stick the incense into the ground, or lean it across your bowl of salted water, so it continues to burn, until the ritual is finished.

Pick up your oil and place a drop on your finger. Anoint your third eye chakra (the space between your eyebrows) with the drop of oil and say,

> *With this oil of divinity,*
> *I bless the divine within me.*

Pick up the fresh flowers. Kneel on the ground before you and say,

> *Unto you,* [insert name of your Higher Power
> or Deity], *I offer these flowers, a symbol of my*
> *love and commitment unto thee. From this*
> *moment forth, I align with thee, and thank*
> *you for your blessings upon me.*

▼ ▼ ▼ ▼ ▼ ▼

Leave the flowers on the ground and let the element of air disperse them, or gather them up and drop them at the base of a tree, or release them into the running water of a creek, stream, or ocean if you live by the sea.

If your incense is still burning, gently put it out in your salted water, then also pour the remainder of the salted water on the ground. Use your incense wand to light other sticks of incense for your rituals or burn as a special offering to your Higher Power. Anoint yourself with the essential oil or perfume whenever you wish to remind yourself of your connection with your Deity.

Moving Forward

The mysteries do not exist in a vacuum. They are fueled with stardust and the ever-changing energies of the universe. Allow yourself to bask in the spirit, be one with nature, spend time gazing at the moon and feeling the warmth of the sun, for every day brings new opportunities to connect with your Higher Power.

The magick is always within you. You are the conduit and the expression. You are the wand of magical smoke and the blessings of light, love, and power.

liGht the cauldron—
workiNG with magick

IN THE EARLY MORNING hours, while the world is still sleeping, an urban Witch rises. She creeps through her house, out into her backyard, carrying her cauldron, incense, and her sacred Book of Shadows, where she stores everything meaningful to her on her journey as a magical, spiritual person. This time is sacred to her, for in these quiet moments of the dawn, she can be with her Deities. In these silent hours of the morning, before the city wakes, she can sincerely enter into sacred space and be in her secret place, where she can share her thoughts, wishes, and desires, as well as her thanksgiving and gratitude.

In the countryside as the moon rises, a solitary practitioner wanders down a familiar road. Her cloak flows silently behind her as her feet carry her to a sacred grove that is well blessed with her presence from working magick there on full moons and holy days. She finds her favorite log to sit upon, allows her cloak to drop, and communes with nature and the Goddess openly, her body being a vessel of love and trust.

Down an alley barely visible to the untrained eye, men and women dressed in white silently slip between painted fences and fragrant magnolia trees. Multicolored beads of purple, green, and gold hang from wrought-iron posts. Spirits greet these people, acknowledging their dedication to ancient rites and rituals. As they quietly step among the cobbled stone and broken sidewalks filled with vines and twisted trunks growing between the cracks, ancestors whisper from trees and leaves blow back and forth, silently welcoming them home to their temple in the city.

All of these people are working magick. They have entered into a state of mind to light the cauldron of spirit and commune with their Higher Powers, Goddesses, Gods, and Deities. They are ready and prepared to shed their clothes of the mundane and don the cloak of magick and spirituality. Their faith and dedication aid them. They know that their commune with nature, the Divine, the Gods and Goddesses, angels, messengers, Orishas, Lwa, and spirit guides is just as true for them living in this day and age as it was for those who have gone before them.

When you commit to working magick and set your foot upon the spiritual cobblestones, the veil parts. The magick begins to take effect, empowering you before you've done one act in the physical realm. The work begins in your soul, in your mind, in the womb of spirit. Your intentions go before you and lay a path for you to follow. Magick begins in your heart.

Working Spells—
Practicing the Art of Folk Magick

Before you do one physical act of magick, see the outcome you desire clearly in your mind. As a spiritual practitioner, I spell the word *magic* with a *k*. The *k* defines magick as a physical and spiritual act, a rite or ritual designed to bring about positive change in one's life, home, or environment. This spelling of magic with the letter *k* separates the rites and practices we do from those who practice "magic" as a sleight-of-hand art, geared more for the stage and theatrical audiences.

Some people say that if we practice magick we don't need to use candles, mojos, or talismans. Some say we don't need spells and incantations, implying we should be able to Conjure up our desires without all this "stuff." Perhaps.

Others say all we need to do is focus our minds and our will shall be done. Maybe. Maybe if you are an adept, one who has walked the ways of the mysteries and practiced the occult for years and years, had the luxury to hermit yourself away in some faraway land, where you can focus one hundred percent on your craft without interruption, maybe then you do your work without "stuff."

But most of us everyday folk need help. We need our candles and incense, our mojos, oils and wands, herbs and plants. We need our Deities, guides, and ancestors to help us Conjure our desires into manifestation. We can't do it alone. Most of us everyday folk need words written down to follow, instructions to emulate, tried-and-true practices to make our own. We need a road, a path to follow. We need a *practice*.

The chapters that follow are the beginning. We will discuss the basics of spell work and delve into the history of African-American folk magick called Hoodoo.

We'll learn how to start adding real magick work to our heartfelt prayers, because in addition to the power of sincere prayers and dedication, working magick is fun. An attitude of craftiness and fun goes a long way in helping you achieve your desired outcomes. Many of us find ourselves at the crossroads of spells, Hoodoo, and folk magick because we grew up believing in lotions, potions, and oils. We watched movies and TV shows about Witches, or believed in ghosts and spirits, or had natural gifts that drew us to the world of the occult and magick.

May the following simple rite and sincere prayer aid you on your journey into magick:

Light a white candle.
Close your eyes.
Say,

> *As above, so below; the magick is with me*
> *wherever I go. What I do and what I say*
> *blesses and guides me along my way. The*
> *way is good, the way is right; may magick and*
> *good juju be with me day and night. By the power*
> *of three times three, blessed be, so mote it be.*

Now that you're all prayed up and in a good state of mind, pour yourself a cup of coffee or tea or make your favorite cocktail. Find a cozy spot, put your feet up, and relax. For now is the time to dive into spell work basics and African-American folk magick known as Hoodoo.

Spell Work Basics

Spells are empowering. Spells are teachers. Spells build confidence and spell work is fun. We often get so bogged down in the right or wrong of magick that we forget that having fun is one of the best energies we can use to empower our magical selves. Many people, including myself, came to the Craft because we loved movies, books, or stories about Witches making potions and charms, crafting spells or stirring cauldrons in the moonlight.

Before we proceed with our first magical working of crafting a mojo, let's spend some time on the basics.

Shush—Don't Tell

"To dare, to will, to know, and to keep silent." This is one of the first rules of working a spell.

We live in a world where sharing is omnipresent. We feel the need to share and tell everything to everyone and anyone. And while sharing is positive, it can also be disastrous for spell work.

I am reminded of a request to participate in a mass spell that was making its way around the internet. The article called for the spell to be a done at a specific time and to let people know if you would be participating in the ritual. In my mind, the spell was already doomed because the whole world knew it was happening and who would be doing it!

There is a reason why some spells, magick, and Hoodoo are done at midnight or in the early hours of the morning. There is no one around! When you work spells, you tap into the energies of the universe and the unseen, calling upon your Deities with sincerity and love to help guide you in your work. Spell work is deep, powerful, personal magick. All magical work should be done with reverence and respect. A rule of thumb I abide by is that one should never call upon entities or Deities they do not understand or respect. Never underestimate the power of the unseen.

Conversely, when you do your spell work, throw your heart, mind, and soul into it! Call upon your Goddesses and Gods, Deities, angels, and ancestors with love and respect, and they will assist you, stand by you, and guide you. What matters most is your sincere heart and good intentions.

When you do spell work, don't share it until you see or know the outcome. You may do some spell work with a trusted group of people; other spell work is more solitary. Some outcomes you may share, some you may never share.

Timing

In Hoodoo, we say do it when you need it. Sometimes you can't wait for the hour of the clock or the moon to be in the right place. You may not be able to wait for the planets to astrologically align in the right zodiac sign. In those instances, you adjust your words to match the cycle you are in.

For instance, if you need to do a prosperity spell during a waning moon cycle, instead of asking for an increase, you would ask for letting go of poverty. If you were working love magick during the waning moon, instead of asking to attract love, you might ask to release loneliness.

If you can plan ahead, there are many different cycles of timing you can use to work magick and Hoodoo. Let's explore some of the basics.

Moon Cycles

When the moon is waxing or growing in size, heading toward a full moon, this is the time to work magick for increasing things in your life. This is a good time for prosperity magick, love magick, and protection magick.

When the moon is waning, decreasing in size after the full moon, this is the time to work magick to let go of things. This a good time to work magick to end harmful relationships, let go of bad habits, or release negativity.

When the moon is dark, meaning you can no longer see it in the sky, this is a time of powerful reflection. I normally abstain from works of magick during this time. Sometimes it is good to wait and reflect on yourself and your intentions during the cycle of the dark moon. Some use dark moon energy to work magick for intentions of a different nature. Just remember to be careful. The line between magick and madness can be very thin!

When the first sliver of the new crescent moon appears in the sky, I take it as a sign to begin working magicks of prosperity and increase. If the skies have been particularly cloudy, as much as it kills me, I will wait until I see the crescent moon in the sky to begin working my magick or Hoodoo again.

Full Moon

The full moon is a time of powerful connections with the Goddess. I was taught that "the moon is full the day before, the day of, and the day after," meaning you have three days to work full moon magick and hold ritual and ceremonies.

I have found the three-day rule to be beneficial. We have to meet life on life's terms. Sometimes you may not be ready for ritual or workings on the exact day the moon is full. Having three days gives you space and time to ready and prepare yourself. While we're on the subject of getting ready, don't feel bad if at every full moon you don't feel like performing a full-blown ritual or acts of magick. In my heart, I believe the Goddess is happy we simply remember her. Sometimes the most powerful magick can be a single candle lit with sincere devotion and intention.

If you choose to work magick on the full moon, know that it gives your magick the most powerful boost possible.

Some spells need to be worked for several days or nights in a row. If you can time your magick to complete it under the light of the full moon, all the better!

Time

Divide your clock from twelve to six and from six to twelve. When time is falling from twelve to six, perform works of letting go or decrease. When time is rising from six to twelve, perform works of attraction or increase.

Seasonal Cycles

The turn of the Wheel offers many days, holidays, and celebrations in which to work our magick. There are solstices, equinoxes, and secular holidays that can be used for spell work.

The summer solstice generally falls on June 21 in the Northern Hemisphere and on December 21 in the Southern Hemisphere. The summer solstice marks the beginning of summer. Although summer is the hottest time of the year, after the solstice occurs the days actually grow shorter and the nights get longer. Summer brings verdant green trees, abundant gardens, and blooming flowers. Use summer energy to work fiery, passionate magick, abundance and prosperity magick, or anything you'd like to see increase.

The winter solstice generally falls on December 21 in the Northern Hemisphere and on June 21 in the Southern Hemisphere. The winter solstice marks the beginning of winter. Although winter may make us shudder, the winter solstice marks the time when daylight begins to lengthen and nighttime begins to shorten.

Even though we are in the darkest time of the year, at the winter solstice we celebrate the return of the light. Our ancestors, who did not have the benefit of electric light, were deeply in tune with the winter solstice. It's not hard to imagine why they appreciated longer days and shorter nights.

The return of the light is a powerful metaphor for overcoming dark times in our lives. Use this time to work magick to bring light into your life. Shine a spotlight in the dark places of your life and know you are a divine magical being. Ride the joy of the holidays and let them infuse your magical workings with faith, hope, and renewal.

In the Southern Hemisphere, seasons are at their polar opposites. The spring equinox in the Northern Hemisphere generally falls on March 20 and in the Southern Hemisphere, the spring equinox generally falls on September 22. Who doesn't love the celebration of spring! The green of nature returns. Our souls and spirits are quickened with the promise of new life. Spring is a great time to work magick for increase, attraction, and new beginnings. Use the energy of spring to awaken dormant parts in your life. Feel the emergence of new life and growth stirring. Let the power of nature infuse your spells.

The autumnal equinox in the Northern Hemisphere generally falls on September 22 and in the Southern Hemisphere on March 20. Autumn is a great time to work magick to celebrate the harvest of projects you planted or began in spring. Autumn is also a great time to perform magick that helps you let go of things no longer needed. You could "magically" clean out your closets by donating clothes to shelters, then smudge your new clean space with some white sage or Palo Santo. You might decide to clean up your garden, do some last-minute weeding, or put away your planting pots and containers as you prepare for the upcoming season of winter.

Our planet is made of polarities. When one season begins in the Northern Hemisphere, it ends in the Southern Hemisphere. Tap into the equinoxes to use the polarities that exist on our planet. Be creative. Let your imagination and creativity fly! We are only limited by our imaginations and our willingness to try new things.

Magick does not exist in a vacuum. You are the creator and manifestor of your works and intentions. You may choose to use all of these timing methods, or none of them. How you time your spells is up to you. There are many opportunities, days, nights, and seasons in which to work magick. Let timing be a guide, an outline, but always remember the power exists within you.

Hoodoo—African-American Folk Magick

What is Hoodoo? Is it Voodoo? Is it a rock formation in the canyons of the southwestern United States? Is it an initiatory practice or can anyone do it? Do I need to be a Christian for my works to be successful? Do I have to learn it from someone in my family? Can I learn Hoodoo in a correspondence class and still perform good and powerful works?

Let's address these valid questions and concerns one at a time.

What Is Hoodoo?

Hoodoo is African-American folk magick. It is born from the folk magick practices of enslaved Africans, most of whom originated from the west coast of Africa and were descendants of the African people known as Yoruba. When enslaved Africans landed on the shores of North America, in the southern region of what is now the United States, they mixed with European peasants and Native Americans who had similar folk magick practices. From this mixing came Hoodoo, a unique blend of ancient and time-honored practices that uses earth elements, roots and oils, fabrics, washes, spirituality, prayers and intention to affect positive changes in one's life.

Workers of Hoodoo are sometimes called rootworkers, aunties, doctors, conjurers, or practitioners.

Historically speaking, a high percentage of people who practice Hoodoo or work for others using Hoodoo are African-American Christian Baptists who use the Bible as their magical text, particularly the Psalms. Hoodoo is also practiced by Appalachian people who live in the Great Smoky Mountains and southern regions of the United States, as well as by a large number of people who live in and around the Crescent City of New Orleans, Louisiana. Hoodoo tends to take on the cultural influences of the region and people who practice it.

In recent times, an explosion of non-African-American people have begun to practice Hoodoo, mostly people of a Pagan or New Age persuasion. These people seek to learn its secrets and add

Hoodoo to their magical practices. However one comes to the practice of Hoodoo, one constant remains: Hoodoo cannot be effectively practiced without the acknowledgement and reverence for the millions of enslaved Africans who carried the remembrances of their pre-Christian lives and magical practices into the New World. Once they arrived on new shores, these people sought roots, foods, fabrics, and materials to continue working their magick while keeping it deeply hidden, sometimes just beneath the covers of Judeo-Christian religions, for fear of death or punishment.

Yoruban culture and people are responsible for the syncretism of religion that eventually became:

- Santeria—Yoruba and Catholicism in Cuba
- Vodou/Vodoun—Yoruba and Catholicism in Haiti
- Shango/Obeah—Yoruba and Catholicism in Trinidad
- New Orleans Vodou—Catholicism, Yoruban, and Haitian influences

If you've been around the magical world for a while or performed spells of Witchcraft, some Hoodoo terms and practices may be familiar to you, including:

- Working with the timing of the moon
- Sewing magical dolls or poppets
- Talismans, also known as mojos, charms, or gris-gris bags
- Using herbs, roots, and oils to affect positive change
- Using symbols or sigils
- Using the tarot or a pendulum for divination

What may not be familiar to you is working in a graveyard, working in the crossroads, using personal concerns (which is a polite name for human bodily fluids, especially ones of a sexual nature; nail clippings; or human hair) or working with altars, all of which are used in a Hoodoo practice.

Is Hoodoo Voodoo?

No. The word *voodoo* is a bastardization of the word *Vodou* or *Vodoun*, which is an initiatory and sacred religion. Vodou originated with enslaved Africans of Yoruban West African ancestries who were forcibly brought to Haiti, Cuba, and the United States, where today it has a large membership of initiates in New Orleans and New York.

The word *voodoo* has entered into the mainstream lexicon to mean anything occult, mysterious, and spell-like. It has also been used to denigrate sincere initiates of a religion that sustained enslaved Africans in their time of deep pain as they crossed the Middle Passage shackled together in chains, surviving torture, starvation, cruelty, and inhuman conditions. The African Diaspora has left its mark upon world religions, music, and culture, as well as the folk magick system known as Hoodoo.

Hoodoo does not follow a rede or dwell upon karmic repercussions. Hoodoo is doing what you need to do when you need to do it. However, as with all spell work, one must be sure their work is justified and take time to perform divination and consult with their Higher Power, especially before working for others or doing spell work of a self-defensive nature. As workers, we always seek to be in alignment with our Higher Power and work within the accordance of the highest good for all concerned parties before we cast any spell, sew any mojo bag, or step into the crossroads or a graveyard.

Know that when you seek to practice Hoodoo, you come into a folk magick tradition whose history is passed down from people who did not have the luxury of going to an attorney or a trusted member of the government to help them when they had problems, needed help, or landed in jail. Hoodoo comes from people who believe in spirit to help them when they have problems with love, a job, protecting their home, watching over their children, and keeping money in their bank account. Hoodoo is down-home, work-it, fix-it, bless-it and let-it-go magick.

Hoodoo and Religion

As Hoodoo has been traditionally practiced by people of Judeo-Christian faiths, one may think if they are not Christian or don't use the Bible as a magical text they cannot perform Hoodoo works.

For any magical practice to be successful, one must align with and work with their Higher Power as it reveals itself to them. One cannot call upon traditions or Gods and Goddesses with whom they are not affiliated or believe in and expect to have successful outcomes. For your magick to work, you must find a way to "put yourself into it"—sage words of advice I was given many years ago by a strong Hoodoo practitioner. To this day, I continue to use her advice in my practices. As I am not a Christian or a Wiccan, calling upon a Higher Power or Gods and Goddesses in which I do not believe or have any association or experience with is counterproductive to my work as a spiritual practitioner.

But where there is a will, there is a way. Where there is sincerity and commitment, and belief in a Higher Power, Hoodoo can and will work for you. Many people get caught up in doubting themselves because they haven't said the magical words just right or they didn't follow the instructions exactly as they were written.

As I stated before, many people who practice Hoodoo use the Bible, particularly the Psalms, as their magical text. When I was a Hoodoo student, I did use the Biblical Psalms at times. However, I never left out my dedication and commitment to the Goddess. As I grew in confidence as a worker, I easily found other texts and prayers that worked for me and aligned with my personal path and beliefs. Nothing is more powerful than a sincere prayer assistance and blessing from your own personal Higher Power. It is the connection to spirit and how you cultivate your relationship with your Higher Power that will be your strongest ally when practicing Hoodoo.

Hoodoo practices also center around working with altars, stepping into the crossroads, and spending time in the graveyard. If you get the heebee jeebees about being in graveyards, you may wish to reconsider pursuing Hoodoo as a magical practice.

Hoodoo also works with *conditions*, which is a term used to connote spell work engaged for life's situations such as prosperity, abundance, success, protection, and love. Hoodoo also incorporates the use of floor washes, baths, and the setting of lights (a term for candle work), as well as dressing and fixing candles for magical work.

Is "hoodoo" a rock formation in the canyons of the southwestern United States?

It most certainly is! Google "hoodoos" and you will find fantastic images of hoodoo rock formations from all over the world. Although rock formations are not used in the folk magick practice of Hoodoo, gazing upon a hoodoo rock formation can indeed be a mystical and magical experience.

Is Hoodoo an initiatory practice or can anyone do it?

No, it is not an initiatory practice, and yes, anyone can do it.

Do I need to be a Christian for my works to be successful?

No, you do not need to be a Christian.

Do I have to learn Hoodoo practices from someone in my family?

Many practitioners come into Hoodoo through a family member or a hereditary lineage. While we all desire to have that great-grandmother, special cousin, or aunt who can teach us magick, sadly many of us don't come from those types of lineages. Hats off to the people for whom magical practices have been passed down from one generation to another. It is indeed special to learn from a member in one's own family line.

In this day and age, however, many are first-time seekers and may not have a trusted and true family member who can teach magick. Thus, this book is intended to be that go-to place. It is intended for those seeking to learn about the hidden mysteries of the occult magick who may not have that special person in their lives to whom they can turn to for practical knowledge.

Can I learn Hoodoo in a correspondence class and still perform good and powerful works?

Absolutely! Just because you are not physically sitting in front of your teacher while they impart their knowledge to you in no way negates your training, especially in this digital age.

The internet abounds with online classes, universities, and tutorials for people to learn anything from fixing their plumbing to achieving bachelor's degrees. A YouTube search will return hours of videos where you can sit and learn about any topic under the sun. Students are home schooled by logging online to connect with teachers and complete assignments. And there are books— countless, wonderful, awesome, magnificent books just waiting to be shared with a reader seeking knowledge.

So why should magick get a bad rap just because you didn't learn at the feet of a wizard? "Hogwash," I say. "Hogwash!"

Put away your doubts and concerns. Sit back, get comfortable, and allow your mind to open as we delve into the world of Hoodoo, altars, and magical spell work.

sacred altar works

ALTARS ARE SACRED SPACES. Altars are places where you come to kneel, pray, and work magick.

Your first altar is the one you create in your mind, by listening to your Higher Power, working with your intuition, and performing rituals. From those rites and practices, you will naturally begin to create physical spaces where you can touch with your spiritual guides and Deities. Those sacred altar spaces will guide you and sustain you in your journey as a magical person.

When I began working Hoodoo, as a magical person I was already familiar with lighting candles, burning incense, and setting up temporary sacred spaces for rites and rituals. Nature and my backyard had always been my go-to places, but once the rite or ritual was over, those spaces returned to their natural functions.

As I continued to grow in proficiency working Hoodoo, it dawned on me I needed a permanent space for my magical and spiritual work. I needed a dedicated place where I could take my mojos and spell work, pray over them to ensure their good blessings, and also touch with my own Deities. As I scoped out room after room in our home, I found an unused private spot (which was a miracle because every nook and cranny in our old house is spoken for), which became my first dedicated altar space. I used that one central space for my prayers, for working Hoodoo, for casting spells, and as a place to center and ground.

As I continued to use one altar for everything, it became apparent I was running out of space! It's amazing how magick seems to attract every talisman and charm, candle and book under the sun and moon. I needed to separate and diversify, albeit separating one central altar into smaller individual altars is not an easy task. It dawned on me why some altars never move from their original locations: an altar space can bloom and blossom to large proportions of its own accord. Also, it can be tough work cleaning up melted candle wax, sorting through myriads of tiny crystals, deciding what to keep and what not to keep, as well as preparing a new space to become an altar.

After all the shifting, cleansing, and cleaning, once I set up separate altars for the conditions that were most important to me, my ability to focus and concentrate on my Hoodoo magick improved. When I worked Hoodoo in distinct and dedicated spaces for conditions such as love as well as maintaining connections with my ancestors and Deities, I saw better results from my work.

And for a time, creating and working separate altars for life's conditions, I created an altar to ensure the success, blessings, and protection of a certain African-American president. I was an altar-creating mojo-workin' mama!

I worked and tended my presidential altar every day for four years. Nothing improves your magical knowledge, skills, and abilities better than working an altar. The time and effort it takes to keep it going by lighting candles, saying prayers, keeping it clean, and performing magick every day returns to you three times three, times three. Tending to an altar is a sincere act of spiritual dedication.

Altars also have a way of spreading and growing like mint in a garden. I've been to spiritual temples where altars took up an entire room. I've walked into altar rooms in China that were filled with larger than life statues of Deities so powerful it took your breath away. I've been to altar rooms in New Orleans, where there are so many papers, candles, statues, mojos, bottles, and offerings on the walls you couldn't tell where the altar stopped and the floor began.

I've also been in homes where the altar was a simple niche in a wall. I've been to religious chapels where people have left offerings of clothes, photographs, prosthetic limbs, dolls, and anything else they felt important to communicate their desires for healing and protection.

But altars don't always have to be large and grandiose. They can be as tiny as one small stone that fits in the palm of your hand. Some of my favorite altars are hidden in plain sight in Asian food restaurants or nail salons. It's not the size of the altar that matters. What is important is when you come to your altar, whether it is large or small, it evokes a sense of connection and reverence.

How to Create a Personal Altar

Have you ever stepped into a grove of trees and heard the call of the Divine? Have you ever sat on the edge of a rock and felt your heart flutter? Or stepped into the night and whispered to the stars?

One must have a sacred space, a private space in which to create, meditate, and work magick. There is a reason why ancient cathedrals and sites of worship exude power and the ability to make the believer and the seeker, believe and know their prayers have been heard and answered.

Power and energy build up in places over time. Just as we use the act of smudging to cleanse and release negativity from a space, a personal altar holds and builds energy from our prayers and the magick we work there over time.

A practitioner may have several altars. Personally, I have more than one altar in my home. Some altars get changed around depending on the season. Other altars remain stationary, while continually being added to with things I deem necessary and power-enhancing to my work.

One of the benefits of having a personal altar is that you know when you sit down at it, it holds your dreams and wishes. It has kept your secrets and the deep wishes of your heart. It speaks to no one, only to you. And if you are truly going to work magick and tap into the spirit world, you need a personal altar space.

I can hear you thinking. How much space do I need? What if I live with people where creating a personal altar isn't practical? What if my fur babies get into the altar and knock it over? What if? What if? What if?

First and foremost, your altar can be as big or small as you desire. It can take up a lot of space or hardly any at all. It can fit in your pocket or it can take up an entire room. One must be practical. We never want to set an altar in a place where others might disturb it or throw bad energy toward it.

If you live in a place where you don't have privacy to create an altar, consider making a small portable one that you can set up whenever you desire to connect with the Divine in a sacred way. You can also hide things in plain sight. A statue, picture, or a flower in a pretty vase can all serve as touch points for sacred work. Lighting a tealight candle in front of those items will help you pray or work with the energies of the Divine. After your work has finished, you can remove the candle and no one will realize the space is your sacred altar.

The goal is to build a practice. There is a reason why the year is marked with holidays, why people go to church every Sunday, or pray every day. One needs to build spiritual muscle. Having a personal altar gives you a place to develop spiritual strength. Your altar works quietly on your mind and intentions whenever you pass it or see it, even if you're not actively working it. It holds your spiritual energy. It calls you, it whispers to you. Your personal altar becomes your friend, your guide, your helper and your tool.

Basic Items for Your Personal Altar

Let's start with some basic things one would have on an altar. Remember these are only suggestions. You may have all of these things or none of them. One of the best things about an altar is that it builds over time.

Some items may stay on your altar at all times. Other items you may switch out or remove as you see fit. The more you work with your sacred space, the more you will come to intimately know and trust what works best for you.

Cloth, crystals, stones, pictures, candles, beads, herbs, oils, wands, mojos, talismans, pieces of jewelry, souvenirs, a journal, fresh flowers, statues, books, matches, heirlooms, tarot cards—all these things can have a place on your altar.

When first starting out, you may find you only need a couple of things in your sacred space. By the nature of working an altar, you will find you tend to accumulate things. I've seen entire rooms filled floor to ceiling with sacred objects, each object and corner being a holy relic.

I've felt the power and simplicity of a simple flower vase in a crevice. I've seen gigantic cauldrons that hold incense which has been lit for centuries. It's apparent we need a space to touch with the Divine and say our prayers. The heart has things it whispers, that can only be shared in private, sacred places.

The first and foremost thing to hold in your mind when creating a personal altar is why you are setting up the space. Is this space going to be used to work spells? Honor your ancestors? Hold precious items? Is this a space where you simply come to pray and meditate?

When I first started creating altars in my home, I had one central spot I used for all of the above. I prayed in that space, worked magick in that space, kept precious things and photos of my ancestors in that space. That first personal altar became a sacred touchstone for me.

Over time as I branched out with different workings, I found I needed separate altars, like my prosperity altar. My prosperity altar lives in a different space than my personal altar. It sits in a space in my home that has been wonderful in generating prosperity for my family, my loved ones, and me.

My personal altar lives in a private space. My love altar lives in another space. My shrine to Gods and Goddesses lives in another space. I'm blessed my family supports me and allows me to have my altars as part of our home. They have come to know the power and presence of a sacred space, dedicated to the Divine.

You may have a different situation and that's okay. It may not be safe for you to have your altars exposed. Remember, the Craft meets you where you are and grows with you. Never jeopardize your safety. There is nothing worse than trying to work magick or pray in places where you are not supported. If your safety or comfort is at stake, you may find your personal altar to be as simple as a small stone or crystal you carry in your pocket that you can easily take out and work with, wherever you are.

The Divine Mysteries are ancient. They call to us. They are always around us. It doesn't matter what size or shape your personal altars become. What really matters is you take the time to honor the Divine within yourself and build a practice. Over time as you grow in your spiritual practice, your personal altars will grow along with you.

How to Create an Ancestral Altar

Death. It hits us hard. The death or passing of a loved one rips our soul, tears our hearts apart, and causes us to weep deep tears.

Death comes to us all. It comes to our loved ones, family members—human and nonhuman, our friends, plants, flowers, trees, and the cycles of our lives.

Death shows up every day. Sometimes death can be a blessing. Death can be a relief if someone or a situation has been long-suffering. Healing can come in the form of death. But however death comes it will surely wrench your heart and tear at your soul, until grieving is over and the light of living dawns upon your days.

We as spiritual people upon the path of magick know death is not the end (a statement that at the time of a beloved's passing sounds good, but can be oh so difficult to put into reality until grieving has passed). In her wisdom, Mother Earth and nature show us daily and seasonally death is not the end.

The sun rises every day. Trees drop their leaves in fall, only to leaf anew in spring. Perennial plants that appear to die return with fresh shoots and flowers when temperatures warm the following season.

In Western culture, we are taught death is something to be scared of, feared, and certainly not honored. In Western culture when someone dies, we hold a service, family and loved ones from near and far attend, the body of the loved one is returned to the earth either through cremation or burial in the ground, and that's pretty much it. Of course family members may keep ashes or photos, but as far as acknowledging the beloved person now on the "other side," on a daily, weekly, or seasonal basis, no actual ceremonies or practices exist.

Cultural Celebrations of Death

But in many cultures on the planet, relegating the passing of a loved one to a onetime service is simply unheard of. In many societies on Earth, the death of a loved one opens the door for ancestral remembrance and altars. Some cultures such as Latino and Hispanic honor their ancestors through the beautiful and touching rituals of Día de Los Muertos and elaborate altars known as *ofrendas*.

In China, ancestors are remembered in home shrines. Traditions also exist where paper money and paper clothes are burned so the ancestors can buy what they need on the "other side," ensuring their loved ones are taken care of in their new lives.

In Haitian Vodou and New Orleans Vodou, ancestors are remembered in correspondence with All Saints Day, in a fantastic ecstatic ritual known as Fet Gede. Fet Gede brings drums, song and dance, altars, crosses, and the Gede—who usually appear wearing tails and top hat, walking with a cane—along with their leader Bawon Samdi, into the realm of the living. At Fet Gede, we dance to the drums of our ancestors and honor the Lwa who guard the cemetery and keep the dead sacred.

Halloween, which is a secular holiday but has grown in tremendous popularity, honors death through spooky, macabre, and sometimes downright scary and monstrous imagery. However, on the other side of Halloween is the spiritual and religious ceremony of Samhain (pronounced *Saw-en*), an ancient ritual of Celtic origin that honors those who have crossed over, allowing us to touch with their spirits and memories when the veil is thin, during the twilight time of October 31.

Samhain altars are lovingly created and gorgeously decorated to honor autumn and our loved ones on the other side. A long-standing tradition of Samhain is the Dumb Supper.

▲▲▲▲▲▲▲▲▲▲▲▲▲▲▲▲▲▲▲▲▲▲▲▲▲

The Dumb Supper–Dinner for the Dead

Items needed:

A black tablecloth

Marigolds

A vase filled with water

A place setting—plate, silverware, napkin and a drinking cup

Some of the favorite foods and drinks of your ancestors

An orange candle

A black candle

A skull candle

Mementos of your loved ones
Matches or a lighter

On Samhain night, cover your table space with the black tablecloth. Place the marigolds in the vase filled with water, and set it on your table. Lay out the place setting and add the favorite foods and drinks of your ancestors.

Place the orange and black candles on the table. Set the skull candle between the orange and black candles. Add your mementos. Light your candles. Take a moment to be with your altar space and your loved ones across the veil. Say any words that come from your heart.

Welcome your loved ones in spirit by saying:

Your presence is welcome here.
If you choose, please draw near.
Out of sight but never gone,
We welcome you here all night long.

▼ ▼ ▼ ▼ ▼ ▼

When the candles have burned down, thank your ancestors for joining you on Samhain night. Return any leftover food and drink to the earth.

Basic Items for Your Ancestral Altar

At the time of Samhain, Día de Los Muertos, or Fet Gede, many will create temporary altars to their ancestors. These altars are fantastic creations of love, time, energy, and effort to honor those who have gone before us. After the ceremonies are over, however, those altars are usually taken down and the precious mementos are returned to their boxes or shelves to be stored until the next year's ceremony or ritual.

By creating a permanent ancestral altar or space of reverence for your loved ones, you can touch with them every day. When the time of remembrance comes in the fall, you can easily port your mementos from your daily ancestral altar to a larger, more elaborate altar you create for the holiday.

You don't need much to set up an ancestral altar other than your love and appreciation and your precious mementos such as photos and keepsakes. Some choose to keep the ashes of their loved ones on their ancestral altar.

You may wish to use a shelf, the top of a dresser, or a closet for your permanent ancestral altar. The point is your altar should be somewhere where you can pass it daily and have a brief moment of heartfelt connection with those who have gone before you. Below are suggestions for spiritual items to add to your ancestral altar.

Florida Water

A highly recommended item for use on an ancestral altar is Florida Water. It is one of the most popular items used in Hoodoo and magical spell work. Many people may be familiar with Florida Water from its time-honored spot on the drug store shelf next to witch hazel. For nearly two hundred years, Florida Water has been extoled as a cooling, healing remedy for the skin, as a refreshing addition to add to your bathwater after a long hot day, or as a spicy, citrus cologne that cleanses and uplifts the body, mind, and spirit.

However, where Florida Water really shines is in its myriad uses in the spiritual realm. Shamans, Witches, healers, and all types of practitioners swear by Florida Water for its ability to clear negative energy, attract good luck, protect one from nightmares, and use as an offering to your ancestors. As a spiritual blessing in liquid form, it can be used daily to anoint one's body to keep the good juju flowing all around you.

Although many homemade recipes abound, the most famous and easily found version of Florida Water is made by Murray & Lanman. Their bottle of Florida Water is easily recognizable by its long neck, foil wrapping, and lovely imagery of flowers, birds, and a flowing waterfall on the label.

Contrary to popular belief, Florida Water is not made in Florida. The name *Agua De Florida* actually means *waters of flowers*. For many years Murray & Lanman have enjoyed a long-lasting relationship with spiritual workers in the Afro-Latino communities. Florida Water shows up on the shelves of priests and priestesses all across Latin America and the United States. It holds a place of honor and respect in ceremonies of initiation, healing, and cleansing.

Some other items you may consider placing on your ancestral altar include the following:

- Sticks of incense and a holder to burn the incense
- Sage bundles
- Candles
- Shells
- Saltwater
- Fresh flowers—to be changed when they have withered
- Sweetgrass
- Palo Santo incense
- Copal resin to be burned on a charcoal disk

- Frankincense nuggets to be burned on a charcoal disk
- Fireproof container to burn charcoal disks and resins

Daily Ancestor Veneration

Our ancestors are important to us. It is upon their shoulders we stand. Creating an ancestral altar and remembering those who have gone before us in your daily prayers is an excellent way to keep the spirit of your loved ones alive and vivid in your heart and memories.

In Vodou, ancestors can be honored with a daily prayer in which we speak aloud the names of those of who have gone before us. We pour libations to them first thing in the morning, before we take our first drink of the day. (It can be difficult and challenging not to take a drink upon rising in the morning, but the discipline you gain through this practice carries you far in your journey as a magical and spiritual person.)

The chapter titled Knock Upon the Magical Door includes rituals for greeting the dawn and smudging our spaces, which can both be done in front of your ancestral altar. I have found performing a prayer for your ancestors fits nicely after doing your ritual for greeting the dawn.

▲▲▲▲▲▲▲▲▲▲▲▲▲▲▲▲▲▲▲▲▲▲▲▲
Ancestor Ritual

Items needed:
A glass of water

Stand facing the direction of east. Close your eyes and think upon the names of your loved ones who have crossed over. I also include the names of our fur family members because the animal beings with whom we share are daily lives are also important members of our family.

Hold the glass of water in your hands and make the sign of a cross in the air. This cross is not a symbol of a religion; rather, it is a symbol of the crossroads, a portal to the other side. Water is the fluid of the spirit. Water carries our thoughts, feelings, and emotions to the realm of our ancestors.

Dip your fingers in the water and throw a bit of the water through the center of the crossroads.

Say these words over your glass of water:

To those who have gone before me.

Now speak aloud all the names of your loved ones who have crossed over.

When you have finished saying the names of your ancestors, pour some water on the ground.

Raise your glass to the sky. Take a moment to feel the love and gratitude emanating from you to your ancestors and from your ancestors back to you.

With gratitude, now take your first sip of water of the day. Give thanks to your ancestors and appreciate the life-giving force of water and the connection it has to you and your loved ones on the other side.

▼ ▼ ▼ ▼ ▼ ▼

Add this ritual to your daily practice and your ancestors will always be alive in your heart, never to be forgotten. This ritual is adapted from *The New Orleans Voodoo Tarot* by Louis Martinié and Sallie Ann Glassman.

Working Your Ancestral Altar

Your ancestral altar will grow at its own speed and volition as loved ones leave the realm of the living for the other side. A daily routine for being with your altar may include lighting sticks of incense, burning resins on charcoal, adding fresh flowers and discarding old ones, smudging your altar, anointing mementos with Florida Water and lighting candles. May your ancestral altar be a source of love and connection, comfort and blessings.

An Altar for Love

Love is fickle. Love is passionate. Love is romantic and lustful. Love is fun, blissful, and exciting. Love can also be exhausting, draining, irritating, annoying, and stressful.

Love can make you angry. Love can make you happy. Love can ruin your day or uplift it. Love is unconditional and conditional. Love is jealous. Love is sneaky. Love is lurid, hot, and weepy.

Love is fleeting. Love is eternal. Love is everlasting. Love is old and love is new. Your love altar is the exact spot to address all these concerns and situations.

You can create a love altar for you and your spouse or one for the family. You can create one to help you love yourself wholly and completely. You can create a love altar to bring new love into your life or to keep an old love fresh and vibrant. One must keep their sexy going! Your love altar can be as diversified or as specific as you desire.

Your first step is to decide where to put the love altar. Is this something you wish to share with your beloved or is this something you'd feel better about working in private? You may need to take baby steps with your love altar. If your beloved is open to the idea, seeing the altar can be a source of fun, joy, and magical stimulation to your relationship. On the other hand, if having the altar out in the open brings unwarranted comments or negative feelings, it's best to keep it in a private space.

The ideas for working a love altar deal with mutual consent and bringing fresh love in a positive way into your life. They are not for coercing people to go against their will in any way. Trying to force someone into your life only brings heartache and headaches. If someone doesn't want to be with you, move on! There are plenty of fish in the sea, and when you feel good about yourself, your ability to attract and manifest love increases a thousandfold.

Basic Items for Your Love Altar

Below is a list of items you can use on your love altar. You may use all of these items or none of them. As you work your altar over time, you will come to know which items bring you the manifested results you seek.

- Red candles

- Pink candles

- Figurative candles—man/woman, man/man, woman/woman

- Genitalia candles—penis candles, vulva candles

- Red glitter

- Sexual toys

- Souvenirs from romantic places, such as matchbooks, napkins, keys, programs, magnets

- Lodestones

- A honey jar—to keep sweetness flowing in your relationship (see directions below)

- Photographs of you and your beloved

- Dried flowers

- Fresh flowers—changed out on a weekly basis; don't keep dead flowers on a love altar

- Personal concerns from you and your beloved—hair, nail clippings, sexual fluids collected from a blissful moment with you and your partner

- Figurines—Pan, Aphrodite, cloven-footed males, winged females

- Heart-shaped symbols, stones, or crystals

- Your favorite perfume or cologne

- Whiskey, tequila or damiana liqueur

- Essential oils—rose, patchouli, frankincense

- A red cloth, box, or tray

▲▲▲▲▲▲▲▲▲▲▲▲▲▲▲▲▲▲▲▲▲▲▲▲▲
How to Create a Love Honey Jar

Items needed:

A medium-sized mason jar with a lid

Honey

Personal concerns from you and your beloved (see below)

A love petition (see below)

Gathering personal concerns can be a magical and romantic way to add magick to your love life. You and your partner can make the gathering a fun exercise. Add snips of fabric from you and your beloved's undergarments. Give your partner a manicure or pedicure and save the nail clippings. Give your partner a scalp massage and save the hair from the brush or comb. The idea is to make the gathering fun and personal.

A love petition is a note that states your prayers or intentions for the work you are doing. I was taught to use brown paper, torn from a brown paper bag, with no machine-created sides, meaning you hand tear each side of the paper so the paper is jagged on all sides.

Fill the jar with honey and add the personal concerns and love petition. Place a bit of the honey on your tongue and say,

> *As this honey is sweet, so shall the love between me and* [insert name] *forever be sweet.*

Seal the jar with the lid. You now have a perfect place to set your dressed and fixed love candles. When you add a candle to the top of the jar, allow the candle to burn completely out, while the wax drips over the lid. Over time, you will have a lovely honey jar that has been blessed with love and good intentions for your relationship. Honey jars are lovely, slow-working spells that build strength and power as you continue to work them.

▼ ▼ ▼ ▼ ▼ ▼

Tending Your Love Altar

The best day of the week to work your love altar is Friday. *Friday* is named in honor of the Goddesses Freya (who is sometimes confused with Frigg), Aphrodite, and Venus. Their mythological prowess and large appetite are legendary.

Fridays are also good days for date nights. Friday signals the weekend and good times ahead. Friday is when 9 to 5 working folks look forward to partying. It's a good day to use the energy of celebration and good times to work your love altar.

Although I suggested Friday as the best day to work your love altar, ultimately your day of choice is up to you. There may be a day of the week that is special to you, or to you and your beloved. The most important thing about choosing a day in which to work is that you be consistent. Decide whether you're going to tend your altar on a weekly or monthly basis. Personally, I tend my altar on a weekly basis to keep my love magick strong. Plus there is so much that can happen in a relationship in just one week!

I also find that in the busy world in which we live, tending your altar may be your only time to work a bit of magick. As you build your altar, over time you'll know which candles to light, incense to burn, and prayers to say, so it won't take you very long to stand before it and do what you need to do. This is good for you as a practitioner and good for your relationship.

Altars love to be tended. They are extensions of your soul and inner beliefs. Have fun with them. Be playful and creative. Allow yourself to be free in your expression of love. After all, this is a private altar, created for you and your beloved and your passion.

Below are some simple rituals to perform at your love altar:

- Light a candle
- Burn incense
- Pour your favorite liquor over your figurines

• Add fresh flowers on a consistent basis

• Write love notes

Love Altar Ritual

When you seek to approach your love altar, do so from the space of presenting yourself at your best, as if you were meeting your lover and you want them to appreciate your loveliness.

Before you light candles on your love altar, allow yourself time to take a luxurious bath or shower. Use your favorite scented soaps, bath gels, or salts or herbal scrubs as you bathe. Concentrate on your beloved and your intentions.

When you've finished bathing, if you feel comfortable doing so, approach your altar naked, or put on clothes that make you feel sexy and attractive.

Light your candle. Think good thoughts for you and you and your beloved. Send good juju love energy out to your loved one. If possible, allow your candle to burn all the way out. And if you're using your love altar to attract a partner, you could light your candle, let it burn for awhile, then pinch it out and continue lighting the candle until your outcome for love is achieved. When it comes to working your love altar, the possibilities are limitless. Have fun with your altar and watch your love magick bloom.

Ritual for Prosperity and Abundance

Through the pages of this chapter you have learned how to create a personal altar, an ancestral altar, and a love altar—sacred works which are important to every magical person on the path of spirituality. However, we cannot conclude without addressing a condition we all deal with in one way or another: the condition of prosperity and abundance.

Many of us arrive upon our spiritual journey from religions or influences that equate poverty with divinity, as a way of being spiritually committed to our Higher Power. Many of us have past life memories of being people for whom poverty and chastity were our signposts of being devoted spiritual people. But that was then and this is now. The world has changed. We need to make money and have incomes to support families and ourselves. There is nothing superior or fun about living in poverty or constantly struggling to make your ends meet. In fact, that constant struggle for income and survival can rob a person of their magical talents and gifts. It is my belief that the universe wants us to succeed. The world is a prosperous and abundant place. Life springs eternal. Your personal altar space is a great place to perform this ritual.

▲▲▲▲▲▲▲▲▲▲▲▲▲▲▲▲▲▲▲▲▲▲▲▲

Prosperity and Abundance Ritual

Perform this ritual when the moon is in its waxing phase, growing from the new moon to the full moon. Also perform this ritual when the minutes on the clock are rising, when time is moving from the half hour (0:30) to the beginning of a new hour.

Items needed:

A green candle

Florida Water

A carving tool or green permanent marker

Prosperity oil or crown of success oil (available
    online or at metaphysical stores)
Olive oil (which can be used in place of the above oils)
Green glitter
Gold glitter
A stick of Palo Santo incense

Cleanse your green candle with the Florida Water. Using your carving tool, carve the word *success* into your candle. If you choose to use a glass-encased candle, you can write the word *success* on the glass with green permanent marker. Anoint the candle with the condition oils or the olive oil. Sprinkle the candle with the gold and green glitter.

All of these items are a signal, a beacon to spirit for your success, which you now are calling to you! Let go of any preconceived notions of lack, less than, not worthy of, or undeserving thoughts. Know you are a child of the universe created with the same atoms and stardust of which the galaxies, stars, and planets are made of!

Invoke Prosperity and Abundance
Light your candle.

Light your stick of Palo Santo. Wave the stick through the air over your candle. Call upon your Higher Power and say,

> *I* [insert your name] *am worthy of prosperity and*
> *abundance. I thank my* [insert name or simply
> say *Higher Power*] *for all the blessings, gifts, and*
> *opportunities I have received, and for all the*

blessings, gifts, and opportunities that are on their
way to me right now. May my every cell be healthy
and well. May I live long and prosper. As I will it,
so mote it be, three times three times three!

▼ ▼ ▼ ▼ ▼ ▼

Allow your candle to burn completely out. Repeat this ritual during every waxing moon cycle to keep the good juju of prosperity and abundance flowing to you.

MAGICAL MOJO
SPELL WORK

What Is a Mojo?

THE WORD *MOJO* HAS come to mean many things. It has found its way into popular culture through songs and music. Jim Morrison made the word famous with the chorus of his song "L.A. Woman" in which he repeats the phrase "Mr. Mojo risin'," which many say was an anagram for his name. Mike Myers gave the word superstar status when his character Austin Powers lost his mojo. Suddenly, everyone needed to have a mojo, and to know what to do if they lost it, or how to recover it if it went missing. We also know prior to Jim Morrison and Mike Meyers using the word artistically, many blues artists sang about mojos and Hoodoo. All one had to do was listen carefully to the lyrics to really know what the song was about.

I Got My Mojo Workin', But How?

True to form, mojos do imbue their owner with powers of protection, love, prosperity, and success. They can be created and charged with countless intentions. They can be filled with many different types of herbs, petition papers, stones, and personal items to bring good luck, power, and success to the owner.

However, in contrast to how the word *mojo* has been used in popular culture, a mojo is a real item, a tangible piece of magick, a talisman, or gris-gris bag you can actually hold in your hand.

Mojos can be made from any type of material, although in African-American folk magick, they are typically made from flannel.

Mojos are also said to attract favorable conditions based on the color of the fabric used. Traditionally speaking:

- Green—attracts the power of money, prosperity, abundance
- Yellow—attracts blessings for safe travel
- Gold—attracts the power for manifesting success
- Red—attracts the power of love and sexual attraction

Rarely have I seen mojos in the color of black or brown. In the section on how to craft a baby blessing mojo later in this chapter, I recommend using the colors of pink or blue, in addition to choosing the color of red, which is a traditional mojo color. But as we become more aware of gender choices and roles, one may choose to add a choice of color they feel is appropriate.

Mojos can also be sewn into little pouches or tied hobo-style. And in today's day and age, premade mojo bags can be purchased online or in metaphysical supply stores. My first mojo, purchased from a spiritual supply shop, was a leather pouch that the maker termed a *medicine bag*. It was filled with fur, bones, stones, and other assorted spiritual items.

People tend to keep their mojos in secret places. A mojo isn't a charm you should willy-nilly show to everyone and anybody. A mojo stores your magick and desires for a specific outcome. Once it is set to workin' (as you will learn how to do in the upcoming sections), you will want to keep your mojo in a safe place. Women sometimes keep their mojos in their bras. Men may keep their mojos in their pockets. You might choose to keep your mojo in a secret drawer or sacred spot, only known to you. Some mojos, as you will learn, stay on an altar until they're ready to work for you. As you work with your mojo, it will become an intimate part of your magick. In time, your mojo may become as valuable to you as any long-cherished piece of jewelry or family heirloom.

As you travel down the folk magick path, you will find that the names of talismans and charms may differ; however, when you get to the root of the condition they were created for, the magical item is essentially the same, for there is nothing new under the sun. Since our arrival onto the planet, humans have had basically the same needs. We need food and shelter. We need love. We need protection and we desire success.

So if someone calls your mojo by a different name, don't be alarmed. It simply depends on where you are from or how your tradition was handed down. At the root of our power is our belief in the ancient ways of our ancestors, who held the mysteries —the sun, moon, and stars—sacred. They learned how to work magick and attract the conditions into their lives that resulted in positive change. They learned how to get their mojos workin'!

Music and Mojo

I've found it helpful to have some magick Hoodoo music playing when I sit down to craft a mojo. By no means is this list complete.

Music is a personal experience. What resonates with one may not resonate with another. But if you're just getting started in the world of mojo magick, it can be helpful to your craft to have some magical musical vibes going, as you sit, stitch, and sew.

Some suggested mainstream musical artists to help you get your mojo workin':

- Beyoncé
- Billie Holiday
- Bruno Mars
- Doobie Brothers
- Dr. John
- Ella Fitzgerald
- Etta James
- Louis Armstrong
- Nina Simone
- Stevie Ray Vaughan
- Wynton Marsalis

If you're interested in adding some zip to your workings, listen to zydeco music. Zydeco music is from Louisiana; it's foot-stomping accordion swing rhythms that set your soul on fire and make you get up out of your seat.

Some suggested zydeco musical artists to get you started:

- Bruce Daigrepont
- Buckwheat Zydeco
- Chubby Carrier and the Zydeco Swamp Band

- Nathan and the Zydeco Cha-Chas
- Sean Ardoin
- Zydeco Joe

And here are some suggested YouTube videos for your additional viewing pleasure:

Sean Ardoin/New Orleans French Quarter Fest 2018

https://www.youtube.com/watch?time_continue=362&v=bdoF02jDzvk

Chubby Carrier and the Zydeco Swamp Band/Zydeco Junkie

https://www.youtube.com/watch?v=H1DxBRvaK50

Conditions

In Hoodoo we refer to situations in life as *conditions*. There are conditions of love, prosperity, protection, health, wealth, and abundance. There are conditions of revenge, sending back, and retribution. In Hoodoo, you do what you need to do, when you need to do it. Working magick with sincere intent is freeing and liberating.

Hoodoo is born from the ancestry of enslaved Africans, Native American Indians, and European peasants, people who did not have the luxury of being able to afford attorneys or certain privileges. Hoodoo is tangible and is rooted in the physical properties of the earth and the mysterious ways of the ancestors. So when these people, who are our ancestors, were in trouble, they turned to their Shamans, wise people, medicine men and women, healers and conjurers, to help them. The ingredients they used in their magical workings were simple and powerful, and were ones the earth readily provided. When the descendants of these ancestors came to what is now known as the United States and to other countries in the world, they quickly learned how to substitute certain roots and herbs, which were similar to ones in their homeland. For example, the use of red brick dust is a substitute for red ochre clay, found in Africa, which is used as a protective barrier from the sun and also as a spiritually protective element.

So when you work Hoodoo, it is into this mindset you must go. This is not high or ceremonial magick. This is the magick of the people, of those who had to turn to ancient ways and remedies, magick and folklore, to protect their homes, families, loved ones, and even their livestock, to survive.

Protective Mojos

Let us work our first piece of Hoodoo, which is to craft a protective mojo. Gather all your materials before you begin to work. Choose a time and place where you will not be disturbed. Nothing breaks a spell like interruptions!

Items needed:

White taper—dressed and fixed with blessing oil or protective oil, then sprinkled with gold glitter (see directions below); matches or a lighter

Florida Water—to cleanse your candle, easily purchased at any convenience store, metaphysical supply store, or botanica

Protection oil—can be olive oil, or a protection oil purchased from a spiritual metaphysical supply shop or botanica

Tool for carving words onto the candle—can be a sharp end of a paper clip, a needle, or even a pushpin. Anything sharp and pointy will do.

Gold glitter

A small piece of plastic wrap to lay your candle on, while dressing and fixing it.

A holder for the candle

A square of red flannel large enough to contain your mojo ingredients

Petition paper—a piece of brown paper torn from a brown paper bag, each side of the paper torn with your hands, leaving ragged edges.

Angelica root

Eucalyptus herb

White thread, knotted nine times

Personal concerns—personal concerns are the hair, fluids, or nail clippings of yourself or the person for whom the Hoodoo is being worked

A Mercury dime—is ninety percent silver and was minted between the years 1916 and 1945. Dimes today are no longer minted with silver, which makes a Mercury dime valuable, as well as a powerful talisman of protection. The wings of Mercury symbolize swift communication, which will add an energetic boost to your prayers for protection.

White yarn, approximately three inches in length

Timing

If possible, this work is best done when the moon is waxing, growing in size from new to full.

Preparation

Dress and fix the candle. These are two terms of Conjure used to ready a candle to be worked for Hoodoo. You will need the white candle, Florida Water, protection oil, the carving tool, gold glitter and the piece of plastic wrap.

First, cleanse the candle. Florida Water is a wonderful cleansing and protective water. Its uses are endless. I use it primarily to cleanse my candles before working with them. Cleansing your candles before working with them removes any negative energy that may have attached itself to the candle. Cleansing with Florida Water also removes the previous energy of anything or anyone who may have touched the candle before you. Because even though candles are delightfully displayed in the shop or online, in reality we know they sat in boxes in warehouses and many hands touched them before ours (unless you're able to make your own candles). This is the primary reason for cleansing your candles before working with them. We need them to be clean for our purposes.

Lay out the piece of plastic wrap, which keeps your work surface clean and keeps the clean energy you are placing into the candle secure. Plus, it makes for easy cleanup.

To cleanse your candle, dip your fingers in the Florida Water and wipe upwards from the center of the candle. Then wipe from the center downwards to the bottom of the candle. Your candle is now clean.

Next, take your carving tool and carve words and symbols of protection into the candle. Use words that are meaningful to you. Your words could be as simple as *protection*, or they could be the name of the person you are making the mojo for; combine words and symbols. There are no wrong or right words. Let your heart and intuition guide you as you carve into your candle.

Once you've carved words into your candle, anoint it using the protective oil. Place a dab of oil on your fingertip and place a bit of oil around the center, the top, and the bottom of the candle. Silently or out loud, say "As above, so below" as you wipe the oil from the center of the candle to the top (including the wick), and then from the center to the bottom of the candle.

Next, lay your candle on the plastic wrap and sprinkle it with the gold glitter. Gold is the color of the sun, the angels, the golden light of spirit. Roll the candle back and forth in the glitter to cover all sides.

Stand your candle upright. Using your fist, knock gently on the candle three times. Tap the candle on the table three times. As you do this, say, "This candle is dressed and fixed for [whomever or whatever protective purpose you are working for]." Set the candle in the candleholder and throw away the plastic wrap. Your candle is now dressed and fixed for this magical Hoodoo working. You will use this procedure over and over again to dress and fix candles for your workings. The only things that may change will be the oils you use and your purpose.

A note of caution—some people like to use herbs in their candles. It has been my experience that herbs catch on fire quite easily. I prefer to place herbs around the base of my candles, while the candle itself sits in a fireproof candleholder. This way, I'm still getting the benefit of the herbs, but the fire danger of the herbs igniting has been brought to nil. We must use our common sense along with our magical sense!

Stitch or tie the mojo. Gather your piece of red flannel. How you choose to use the fabric is up to you. Some people simply place their ingredients on the fabric and tie it up like a hobo bag. Others sew the sides and top of the fabric to make a small mojo bag. I am in no way a seamstress or a tailor, but I can hand stitch a mojo bag. I love how sewing the sides and top infuses each stitch with my magical power and intentions. Others may choose to purchase a premade mojo bag, which saves on time. It is up to you! Use whichever method feels right to create the mojo bag. Once you have your mojo fabric ready for its ingredients, set it aside next to your dressed and fixed candle.

Write a petition paper for protection. Write your prayer of protection on your petition paper. These could be words from your favorite prayer or heartfelt words you create yourself. You could invoke archangels in the prayer. You may write out a prayer to your Deities and ask them to protect you, or the loved one for whom you are working. As long as the prayer is sincere, the words will be appropriate. Write words that bring you solace and comfort.

Once you've written the words on the paper, anoint the paper with the protection oil in a five-spot pattern. A five-spot pattern begins in the top left corner, going clockwise to all the corners of the paper, and ends with a dab of oil in the center of the paper.

After you have anointed the paper, add the angelica root, eucalyptus herb, and any personal concerns to the center of the paper. Fold the paper towards you until you have a nice little packet. Tie it securely with the knotted white thread, which has been knotted nine times. Set your packet aside.

Cleanse the Mercury dime. The last task to do before you put everything in your mojo, is to cleanse your Mercury dime with Florida Water. (If you're wondering where to get a Mercury dime, check with your local coin shop.)

Add the Mercury dime and your petition packet to the mojo. Light your dressed and fixed candle.

Putting It All Together

Light your dressed and fixed candle. Take a deep breath and focus your thoughts on protective energy. See the prayer of protection you have written in your mind's eye. Feel the strength of your Deities you have called upon.

Release your breath into the mojo bag. Feel your prayers and intentions infusing the mojo with protection. Tie the bag shut with the white yarn. Hold the mojo in your hand and speak out loud your prayer of protection, then pass the bag through the candle flame three times and anoint the bag with the protective oil.

Set the mojo next to the candle and allow it to remain there until the candle has burned out.

Once the candle has burned out, your mojo is ready to be used by you or for the purposes for which it was created.

From time to time, depending upon how often you use your mojo, you may find it needs to be fed, or given an energetic boost. To do so, dress and fix a candle the same way you did when you first created the mojo. Say a prayer of protection over the mojo, pass it through the candle flame, anoint the mojo with protective oil, and let it sit before the candle until the candle burns out. This feeding technique works for mojos of all different conditions.

Should you find your mojo becoming tattered after years of use, you can choose to make a new mojo and include the tattered old mojo inside the new one. Or you can bury the old mojo in your backyard or in a flowerpot, to keep the protective energy around you and you loved ones.

As you craft and create mojos over time, you will come to know your favorite herbs, roots and oils that give you the best results. It's not necessary to load a mojo bag until it's overflowing. Sometimes the simplest and fewest ingredients work best, especially if you're just starting out in the world of Hoodoo, magick and Conjure.

Love Mojos

In the chapter titled Sacred Altar Works, you learned how to create a love altar. Now that your love altar is up and running, let's create a love mojo that you can carry with you, or place under your bed or pillow, to attract love into your life or keep the love you have fresh and vibrant.

Many of the same ingredients you used to create your love altar can be used in your love mojo. The only difference will be that instead of placing the items on an altar, you will place them in a red flannel mojo.

Items needed:

A red candle with matches or lighter

Florida Water

Carving tool

Rose essential oil

Frankincense essential oil

Red glitter

Two small lodestones

Whiskey

Lodestone grit

Petition paper—brown paper with torn edges on all sides

Dried rose petals

Personal concerns—hair and nail clippings

White thread knotted nine times

A square of red flannel or a premade red mojo bag

White yarn

Timing

Begin this work on a Friday, during a waxing moon, and choose a time and a place where you will not be disturbed. There is nothing worse than doing spell work and being interrupted as you get into the flow. It takes a strong will and determination to keep going once you have been disturbed. However, a true practitioner, having gained skill over time, will always keep going until the results they desire manifest.

Preparation

Before you begin crafting your love mojo, take a bath or shower. Anoint yourself with your favorite romantic scent (if you have one), light a candle, and put on something sexy. If you have a favorite song or tunes that put you in the mood, play them softly in the background.

Cleanse your red candle with Florida Water. Carve any words into the candle that speak to your heart about the love you wish to bring into your life, or words to keep the love you have vibrant and strong. Anoint the candle with the rose and frankincense essential oils. Roll the candle in red glitter and set it aside.

Gather the two lodestones. If you are in a relationship, you can name the lodestones for you and your beloved. If you are seeking to bring new love into your life, you can name one lodestone for yourself and simply call the other lodestone *my beloved*. Hold the lodestones in your hand. Take a deep breath and visualize your intentions for love. Breathe out your intentions over the stones. Anoint the stones with whiskey, sprinkle lodestone grit over them and set them aside.

Write a petition paper for love. On the brown paper, write your petition for love. Go into your heart and sincerely write out your desire for a new relationship, a continued relationship, or a better relationship between you and your beloved. When you have finished writing your petition, anoint the paper in a five-spot pattern with the rose essential oil. Add a few pinches of rose petals to the center of the petition paper. Add your personal concerns. Fold the paper toward you until it resembles a small packet. Tie the paper with the white thread that has been knotted nine times. Set the packet aside.

Putting It All Together

Gather your red flannel. Light your red candle.

If you are using a premade mojo bag, place the anointed lodestones and petition packet inside the bag. If you are simply going to tie the bag hobo style, lay the lodestones and the petition packet on the square of flannel. If you've stitched your own bag, place the lodestones and petition packet inside the bag.

Once all the items are inside the bag, sprinkle a few more pinches of rose petals inside the bag. Hold the bag in your hand, say a prayer for your love to be manifested in accordance with the highest good for all, breathe into the bag, and pass it through the candle flame three times. Tie the bag shut with the white yarn and anoint it in a five-spot pattern with the frankincense essential oil.

Place the bag on your love altar and leave it there until the red candle burns out. Once the candle has burned out, carry the mojo with you or place it under your bed or pillow. Anytime you feel the mojo needs to be fed (or charged), dress or fix another red candle, light the candle, pass the mojo through the flame three times, and allow the mojo to sit on your love altar until the candle burns out.

A Mojo Story

Ten years ago, a safe travel mojo was one of the first mojos I ever made (the next section shows you how to make your own). They meant a lot to me, as at that time my beloved husband traveled extensively for work. Seems like our love was a series of never-ending hello kisses and tearful goodbyes. But every time he left for the airport, I knew he had his safe travel mojo with him and that he would return to me.

Fast forward to the summer of 2017 when my husband and I made an arduous trip to Europe. During our stay, my hubby became severely ill, and in a tense cab ride through hectic London town, I left my backpack in a black London cab. (Thankfully, my husband recovered from his illness and is doing quite well.)

Although I had my passport and travel documents with me (thank goodness), my backpack had everything else in it, including my safe travel mojo. Dejected, I sat numbly on the couch in our London room, staring blankly at the high ceiling and white painted walls.

"What good was my safe travel mojo if I left my backpack in a cab?" I cried aloud as I frantically searched for a way to contact the cab company. London was the final leg of our journey and we were worn out. I didn't feel I had the strength to go through the hassle or process of getting my backpack returned to me.

Thankfully, I was able to file a claim online for my backpack but was cautioned that it could take days, maybe weeks, for a valid response and we were due to fly home in two days.

It's okay to doubt. It's okay to question your practices and beliefs in times of need and struggle. I believe any normal and sane person goes through periods of doubts about things they profess to believe. It's only human to question and wonder if what you believe will hold true when life gets heavy handed. And I also believe sometimes the universe hands you situations to test your beliefs, to see if what you say or profess is true.

As I sat numb on the couch, wiping tears from my eyes, there came a knock upon the door. It was our London cab driver. He'd found my backpack in his cab and returned it to me! I began to cry, to which he said, "This is what London cabbies do."

I have never been so grateful or so grounded in the power and strength of my safe travel mojo and in my beliefs and practices. We still carry the original safe travel mojos I made for my husband and myself in 2008. I've also made safe travel mojos for others, and they too have found them to be successful in helping them have safe travels.

Safe Travel Mojos

I cannot take credit for safe travel mojos, or the prayer for which you say over them once they are made. For that, I must give gratitude to Cat Yronwode, my Hoodoo teacher, who originally published how to make a safe travel mojo on her site, www.luckymojo .com/safetravel.html and has graciously given her permission for her safe travel prayer to be reprinted within these pages.

You will see within the prayer there is a line that reads, "In times of need may kindly strangers come to [their] aid without stint." No line was truer for us than when the London cabbie returned my backpack to me.

When I sit down to craft safe travel mojos, I pour myself a bit of whiskey and play some jazz music. The whiskey and jazz just seem to lend themselves to a successful Hoodoo-creating-craft mood!

Items needed:
   Comfrey root
   Safe travel oil—available at LuckyMojo.com
      or metaphysical supply stores
   Petition paper—brown paper with torn edges on all sides
   White thread knotted nine times
   Anchor charm
   Yellow flannel
   Pinch of dried mint
   Indian head or Scout cent—bears the face of a
      Native American man wearing a head dress
   White yarn
   Yellow four-inch chime candle—dressed with safe
      travel oil and gold glitter
   Matches or a lighter

Timing
Although a safe travel mojo can be made anytime, the best time to make it is a week to ten days before one departs upon their journey.

Preparation
Dress the comfrey root with safe travel oil.

Prepare the petition for the traveler by writing out the safe travel prayer on brown paper. Below is the safe travel prayer:

> *May* [full name of person] *travel safely*
> *and freely upon the earth, over the water and under the*
> *sky. May no enemy hinder their journey. May no wild*
> *animals beset* [him or her]. *May* [he or she] *find food,*
> *drink, and safe shelter in abundant measure every day. In*
> *times of need, may kindly strangers come to* [his or her]
> *aid without stint. As the peregrine to the nest, may* [full
> name of person] *return home in good speed, having*
> *accomplished all* [his or her] *works successfully*
> *and with complete satisfaction.*

Anoint the petition in a five-spot pattern with safe travel oil. Enclose the comfrey root in the paper and tie it with the white thread. Once your packet is complete, set it aside.

Attach the anchor charm to the yellow flannel mojo bag. Place the petition packet, mint, Indian head or Scout cent in the mojo.

Putting It All Together

Light the dressed yellow candle. As the candle burns, speak aloud the prayer for safe travel. When you have finished saying the prayer, breathe into the bag, tie it shut with the white yarn, anoint the bag with safe travel oil, and pass it through the candle flame three times. Allow the bag to lie beneath the candle until the flame burns out. Once the candle has burned out, your safe travel mojo is ready for travel!

If you are an avid traveler or if you make these for others, use the same space to light your safe travel candle, each time you dress and feed your candle or make a new safe travel mojo.

I light a new yellow candle, dressed and fixed with safe travel oil and gold glitter, each time my husband and I travel by air, or take a long, extended road trip. And in between those feedings, I try to never leave home without my safe travel mojo. The sweet little spot I've used for years to bless our safe travel mojos is now lovingly piled with yellow candle wax and gold glitter. No wonder the force is strong with our safe travel mojos!

May the force be strong with you and your travels, as you see the world blessed with the strength and power of your safe travel mojo.

Baby Blessing Mojos

Few things are more precious than the birth of a child. As a magical worker and practitioner, you may be called upon to craft a mojo for a baby, a newborn beautiful spirit who has just entered the world.

I keep baby mojos pure and simple. In my mind, I keep the parents forefront, not wanting to add any stress to their lives by crafting something they think could be potentially harmful to their child. We are Witches after all, and we never want to give out the message of harming other people. It is an honor to be asked to craft a mojo for a baby, so I take the crafting of it very seriously.

Items needed:
    Pink, blue, or red flannel
    Motherwort herb—brings in protective
        blessings of the Divine Mother

Angelica root herb—smells so lovely and
     brings in angelic vibrations
Mercury dime—for protection
Petition paper—brown paper with torn edges on all sides
Olive oil or blessing oil—to dress the petition paper
Frankincense essential oil—to dress the mojo
White yarn
White thread knotted nine times
A white candle dressed and fixed with frankincense oil,
     blessing oil, and gold glitter

Timing

In Hoodoo we say, "Do it when you need it" (meaning you don't need to wait for conditions to be absolutely perfect for your work); however, when I craft a baby blessing mojo, I wait until the moon is in her waxing phase, growing from new moon to full moon. I also make sure I'm not crafting the mojo on a void-of-course moon day, when the moon is in between astrological signs, because that can add wonkiness to your spell work, and things definitely may not turn out as you intended.

Preparation

Sew your mojo bag using the flannel color of your choice or use a premade mojo bag. Be sure to smudge the premade bag before you fill it, so it is released from any potential negativity and the energies of those who handled the bag before you.

Dress and fix your white candle and set it aside.

Write out your petition paper with your prayers of good intentions for the child. Dress it with the blessing oil and fold the paper towards you. Tie it with the white thread and place it in the mojo.

Add the herbs and the Mercury dime to the mojo.

Putting It All Together

Light the white candle and hold the mojo in your hand. Say a prayer of good intentions and blessings for the child. Breathe those good intentions into the bag and close it shut with your hand. Pass the bag through the candle flame three times. With the frankincense oil, anoint the bag in a five-spot pattern (starting in the left corner continuing clockwise, then finishing with a dab of oil in the center). Tie the bag with the white yarn and allow it to sit before the candle until the candle burns out.

Once the candle has burned out, your baby blessing mojo is ready for gifting.

PROTECTION MAGICK

NOW THAT WE'VE PRACTICED working at our altars and learned how to make mojos, it's time we address Hoodoo to use when life gets hard and we feel we need more than a candle and a prayer.

In short, it's time to talk about going to the crossroads and working in the graveyard, doing what you need to do, when you need to do it.

Let's take a step back and talk about the history of why people have sought their rootworker, Witch, priestess, or conjurer. Sometimes life gets tough. Sometimes you find yourself in situations where you need to call on the power of the universe and your Deities to stop the madness, especially when it's affecting you and your family.

It doesn't take much for a practitioner to understand that the folk magick described in this book comes from the heart of people who in times of deep trouble could not turn to authorities to help them.

We can never be sure of the outcome when we set upon these types of protective works, but it is empowering to follow up your prayers with actions that will aid in a successful outcome to your situation. Bear in mind, especially when doing works of this nature, that we pray for a successful outcome in accordance with the highest good for all involved in the situation.

On the following pages are works that take courage, hutzpah, and commitment. As with all good magick, the adage of "To dare, to know, to will, and to keep silent" is paramount. You may only wish to discuss what you are doing with the people involved, your priestess, priest, or Shaman. But don't talk about your protective work before it's happened or while you're waiting to see the outcome; for nothing ruins a spell quicker than talking or sharing about it, once the spell has been set to workin' and you're waiting for results.

A note about results: magick and Hoodoo take place in the realm of spirit. Once you've done your humanely best as a magical, spiritual person, worked your spell or rite, leave it alone. Don't go back and check, dig it up, or throw the whole thing out before you've given it time to work.

In Hoodoo, we subscribe to the rule of three. Give your spell three days, three weeks, or even three months before you decide it's been successful. Things may just be starting to gel spiritually when you as a human being decide nothing is happening or your spell didn't work. Before you give up on your spell, consider what a good outcome would be for your work. A successful outcome may be that you feel better and your burden has eased. A lift in the lightness of your being is always a good sign you've done good work.

Now that we are armed with our magical parameters, let us raise our magical shields and work some protective magick!

It's Okay to Protect Yourself

Talismans, mojos, salt, and Florida Water. Candles, pentacles, and pentagrams. Jewelry, baubles, spells, and graveyard dirt.

Vèvès, crosses, crucifixes, saltwater, cornmeal, seals and bones, and also prayers, chants, songs, petitions, and sage.

All of these are at your disposal to use in your defensive magick arsenal.

As with most everything you want to do well, practice your defensive magick and take it one step at a time before you move on to another level. Some protective skills and objects may even require an initiation of sorts before you feel confident to use them. Just as trees and roses grow thorns, grow your own defenses, and know that it's okay to protect yourself.

When I work defensive magick, it comes from the standpoint of keeping away, pushing away, sending back things or situations that seek to harm me, my family, or loved ones. It's not about taunting people, a desire to harm others, bragging, or boasting. I find those viewpoints off-putting and disrespectful. No one likes a bully and no one wants to be bullied. And sure enough, when people set about working defensive magick from those perspectives, the magick can definitely return to them in harmful ways they may not have expected!

So let us be clear as we carry on. The following work and spells come from a place of self-defense, love and protection, and doing no harm to others. They are worked only to protect one's home, spaces, friends, family, or loved ones from untoward and ugly situations that simply won't abate without some type of higher, intensive intervention.

If you find yourself wanting to work acts of defensive magick to bully and intimidate others, this isn't the place for you, nor do I support or endorse your endeavors.

Working in the Crossroads

As a Hoodoo student, one of my requirements for a successful certificate of completion was to do work in a crossroads, and would you believe the first place I did crossroads work was in the busy, bustling, old city of Philadelphia! I can still see the intersection in my mind and clearly remember the exciting, surging fear and wonder as to what I was about to undertake.

I'd never done any work in a crossroads before that morning in Philadelphia. Through my studies, I had learned a crossroads is any place two roads meet and form a cross. I'd also learned railroad crossings are powerful crossroads—but we'll talk about that later.

On that early morning in Philadelphia, as I prepared to do my first crossroads work, I became keenly aware of the effort it takes to practice folk magick while living in these modern times. It became crystal clear to me that a lot of the works we do as practitioners originated from a time and place where graveyards were unlocked and a crossroads was literally just down a country road.

When you commit to doing work in a crossroads, the work will require you to either leave your house before the crack of dawn or be in position at the stroke of midnight, which can be thrilling and also a bit scary! But you didn't think it was going to be easy, did you?

Real magick, sincere magick, takes time, effort, and courage, and I have faith in you. If you're reading this book, I know you already possess the fortitude and strength to do this work, or you wouldn't be here. All you need to do is practice.

Below are some tips to help you before you set out to work in a crossroads:

- Scope out your intended crossroads before you decide it's your place for your work. Take time to look around and see what surrounds the crossroads, be it houses, stores, bushes, or trees. Give yourself time to prepare for the work you are about to do.

- Make sure you have all the ingredients for your work before you leave home. Check and double-check your list of magical items.

- A steadfast rule for working in the crossroads (and the graveyard too), is always go home by a different route from whence you came, and don't look back. Going home by a different route prevents any untoward spirits from following you. Not looking back is your statement of faith that spirit is working upon your request. It can be difficult not to look back as you drive or walk away, but don't do it!

- Finally, when you get home, take time to make notes about your experience in your magical journal, Hoodoo journal, or Book of Shadows. As you gain in experience, you'll want to look back on your work and your progress. Also, it's good to keep notes on the outcome of your work. Did it work, did it not? How did you feel when you were doing it? What messages or insights did you receive? It's good to keep in mind how we determine success, and how spirit determines success. Many times, a successful outcome in the realm of spirit may not match with what we believe are successful works. It's our job to trust and work with the answers we are given. Once you've done your best, let it go.

Below are some types of works practitioners do in a crossroad:

- **Disposal**—If you see a brown paper bag lying in the middle of the street, don't pick it up. A crossroad is a portal for letting go of negativity. Many workers toss things they no longer need or want around them into a crossroad. It wouldn't be unusual for some practitioners to leave works of a baneful nature in a crossroad, so if you see a bag lying in the middle of an intersection, leave it be!

- **Cleansing**—One of the simplest and most powerful works done in a crossroads is a ritual cleansing. A cleansing releases things that no longer serve you, from your emotional, physical, or spiritual being. It can be an exhilarating experience to perform a cleansing at the crossroads. I share a cleansing crossroads ritual in this chapter.

- **Assistance in performing a work of art or magick**—Many people have heard the song by Robert Johnson, about how he went down to the crossroads. There's even a great movie about that legend. Much lore abounds about meeting the "black man" at the crossroads who will help you in your task if you have the courage to stay and meet him.

    I've been to the crossroads at midnight, to meet whatever spirit had in store for me as a magical worker. I didn't meet a "black man," but spirit did send me messages that let me know I was definitely not alone and that my petition had been heard. What I gained from going to the crossroads at midnight was courage, strength, tenacity, and wisdom.

Not all crossroads work is performed where two roads meet, forming a T. A railroad crossing is also a powerful place for performing crossroads work. Plus, when you look at the sign above the railroad track, it says *crossroads* where the words *railroad* and *crossing* intersect.

Placing your work on a railroad track in order for the train to run across it and destroy it is powerful work! Of course, if you attempt to do this work, please, please be careful! Scope out the track and what's around it before leaving your mess for the train. The safest way to perform railroad crossroads work is to leave your work upon the track when no train is in sight, or throw your work out the window of your car as you drive over the railroad crossing.

Working in the Graveyard

I have a soft spot in my heart for graveyards. I find them to be places of peace, wonder, history, magick, lore, and mystery. There's been many an afternoon and night I've spent there washing away my tears, soothing my soul, burying spells, or paying homage to spirits who have blessed me and my loved ones with their guidance, strength, and protection.

Many graveyards were intentionally built as parks, where people could sit or stroll as they coped with their grief or find a respite from the trials of life. Not all graveyards are spooky, haunted places, although, as New Orleans calls them, they are "Cities of the Dead," and as such they deserve our respect and honor, especially if you're going to do work in them.

As a Hoodoo student, I was required to dig graveyard dirt, sift it, and send it to my teacher. Digging graveyard dirt is one of those things you either do or do not do. There is no in-between, no substitution. Graveyard dirt is powerful juju. I use it for protection and defensive spell work.

One must remember that in times of old, people's loved ones and ancestors were buried in graveyards close to their homes. They knew exactly where their ancestors were buried and most likely the graveyards weren't locked at night.

Nowadays, doing work in a graveyard can be tricky (and illegal! Please do your research). You'll need to plan ahead where you'll be able to do your work, unless you're blessed with rural graveyards and cemeteries nearby, or are blessed with knowledge of where your ancestors are buried and can work directly with their spirits, should you choose.

I've learned a couple of things about working in graveyards. First, an attitude of reverence and respect is a must. Graveyards and cemeteries are holy, sacred places. They are the sacred burial grounds of family, friends, and loved ones. Treat the graveyard as you would want someone to treat the final resting place of your loved ones.

Second, whenever you pass through the gate, throw some coins to the spiritual gatekeepers of the cemetery or graveyard. There are benevolent spirits who guard the gates, and you always want to be in their favor, especially if you are going to the graveyard to do work.

Third, when you have finished your work, always go home by a different route and don't look back (just like in the crossroads). You have done what you came to do, now leave it there and have faith spirit will intercede and assist you per your request.

Finally, don't tell anyone about the work you have done in the graveyard until you are satisfied with the outcome. I know in this age of sharing everything it can be tempting, but don't do it. Wait and see how your work manifests.

Working in a graveyard can be taxing, exhilarating, and terrifying as well as some of the most powerful work you will ever do. It will thrill you, heal you, uplift you, and drain you. You will need some downtime after working in a graveyard. I always feel a great charge when I'm done, and then I need some simmer down time, some quiet and solitude to collect my thoughts, make notes, and recharge. Which is why when I feel it's time to do work in a graveyard, I've come to that decision soberly. Graveyard work is not for the faint of heart, nor for the callous or lackadaisical practitioner. Respect the graveyard and it will respect you.

How to Gather Graveyard Dirt

Many people have access to where their ancestors and loved ones are buried. This is the best option for gathering graveyard dirt. When you pass through the gate of the cemetery, be sure to throw a few coins to the spiritual gatekeepers of the dead. This is your admission as a spiritual worker and acknowledgment to spirit of the sanctity of the graveyard.

When you approach the grave of your ancestors, find a comfy spot and tell them of your troubles. Ask them to help you with your plight, then gather some dirt from their grave—a small amount will do, such as a tablespoon's worth. Graveyard dirt is powerful. There is no need to gather large amounts. Leave an offering of their favorite foods or drink in return for their assistance. Cover up the hole you dug with dirt, leaving everything intact as you found it.

Once you get home, sift the graveyard dirt to remove any stones or twigs. You now will have blessed graveyard dirt from your ancestors or loved ones for which to do your work.

If you don't have a graveyard nearby where your loved ones or ancestors are buried, two other options are available to you.

Many cemeteries and graveyards have a special spot set aside for soldiers and veterans. These people bravely gave their lives for their country. If working with the graveyard dirt of a soldier calls to you, but you don't know which one, when you enter the graveyard ask to be directed to the grave of the soldier who is most willing to help you. Once you've received your answer, make your way to the soldier's grave. Sit by their grave; tell them of your plight. Ask permission to take some of their graveyard dirt. If you feel a connection, take a small amount of dirt from the grave. Leave a silver dime on the soldier's plot (as payment) and promise to return and honor the soldier's grave for helping you.

Don't make promises you can't keep! If you know you won't be able to return and place flowers on the soldier's grave after the work is done, it's best not to ask for their help. The dead take our requests very seriously!

If you don't feel called to work with the graveyard dirt of a soldier, you can visit the grave of someone who did good works of protection while they were alive. The website www.findagrave .com lists millions of cemetery records upon which to search. You may find a willing connection through this method.

Lastly, you can always enter the graveyard or cemetery and ask spirit to direct you to a person willing to help you in your time of need. If you go this route, spend some time with the person's grave. Look them up to see why the two of you are connected. Once you decide this is the person to help you in your time of need, the same practice applies. Tell them of your troubles, ask for their help, and take a bit of their graveyard dirt. Leave an offering and promise to return and honor their grave once your work has been completed.

Uses for Graveyard Dirt

Once you've gathered your graveyard dirt, use it as a protective agent around your home, place it in mojos, or use it as an offering on your ancestral altar.

To place graveyard dirt in a mojo, sprinkle the dirt in the bag before you close it, or add it to your petition paper before you seal it.

To place graveyard dirt on your ancestral altar, use graveyard dirt you have gathered from your ancestor's grave. Place the dirt in a lovely container, one you feel your ancestors would appreciate, and place it on your altar. From time to time when you spruce up your altar, take the graveyard dirt and disperse it outside your home to keep the spirit of your ancestors with you at all times. (See the section titled Spell Work—How to Protect Your Home or Office Space for a discussion on using graveyard dirt as a protective agent around your home.)

In closing, I'd like to share a little ditty I wrote about working in graveyards. May it bring you comfort and strength when you step onto the sacred ground of a graveyard to perform protective magick:

> *Let's go down to the graveyard and sit a spell.*
> *Leave your troubles with the trees and stones,*
> *They'll never tell.*
> *Dig it*
> *Scratch it*
> *Bury it in the dirt*
> *Put an end to your pain, your troubles, and hurt.*

Spell Work—Wash It Away in the Crossroads

This is a simple and powerful spell to release negativity as you take a shower or bath.

Items needed:

Two white tealights or glass-encased candles
Matches or a lighter
Florida Water
A container
1 cup sea salt, Himalayan salt, or kosher salt
¼ cup olive oil
½ lemon, from which the juice has been squeezed
Clean fresh clothes

Timing

Arise early in the morning before dawn. Speak to no one.

Preparation

Cleanse your candles with the Florida Water, light them, and set them outside your bath so you can step between them when you have finished bathing.

Gather the salt, olive oil, and lemon. Bless them with these words:

Blessed be element of salt.
Blessed be healing properties of olive oil.
Blessed be healing, cleansing properties of lemon.

Combine the salt and olive oil in a container that you can easily hold in your hands. Place the lemon on top of the mixture. Carry the container with salt, oil, and lemon into your bath.

Prepare to take a shower or bath. Give thanks for your water as you rinse your body.

Use the lemon to gather the oil and salt mixture from the container. Scrub yourself lovingly with the salt and olive oil, using the lemon as a scrubby. Visualize washing away negative feelings and emotions. Be careful not to get the mixture into any cuts or other sensitive parts of your body.

Rinse off and keep some of the rinse water.

Step from your bath between the two candles. Allow your body time to air dry and put on clean clothes. Pinch out the candles.

Putting It All Together

Carry your rinse water to the crossroads. Step into the crossroads with your back to the direction of east. Throw the rinse water over your left shoulder with force, so you hear it hit the ground. Thank the crossroads for taking your negative feelings and emotions from you. Step out of the crossroads, don't look back, and return home by a different route from whence you came.

When you get home, dispose of the used lemon in the trash, preferably in a receptacle outside your home.

Spell Work—How to Protect Your Home or Office Space

Gargoyles, owls, prickly plants, railroad spikes, security systems, dogs, fierce cats, motion detectors, and locked gates and fences are just a few of the things we use to protect our homes and families from intruders. You can also use the following spell work to help protect your home or office dwelling.

Red Brick Dust

Red ochre is the color of clay found in many parts of Africa. African people use red ochre as a protective shield on their bodies and homes. When enslaved Africans landed in Louisiana, they found a substitute for red ochre: red brick dust.

Lay red brick dust across your threshold as a protective measure to keep unwanted persons away. If you don't want folks to know red brick dust is on your threshold, put it under a doormat. Combine red brick dust with graveyard dirt and add protective herbs such as eucalyptus or angelica root. Grind everything together and use the mixture as your own protective threshold powder.

Railroad Spikes

Railroad spikes add the energy of iron to nail down your property to keep your things from being taken.

Push railroad spikes into the soil around the four corners of your property. Plant the spikes in flowerpots and set them around your property. As you set the spikes into pots or push them into the soil around your property, say a prayer of protection to your Deities. Thank them for protecting your property through the power of the railroad spike.

Gargoyles

Flying winged creatures of stone! Humpbacked caricatures baring their teeth! Dragons and grotesque faces. They're fun, they're cute, they're hideous, and they make great protectors.

You can find many of these wonderful creatures on the internet. When gardening season comes around, check your local garden store. You will find many of these stone beings hidden among the plants and flowers, just waiting to go to a good home.

Gargoyles originate from medieval times when they were used as water spouts on buildings. Perhaps their hideous faces kept people from siphoning water or destroying property. In light of their original intention, gargoyles can be joyful little creatures to place around the outside of your home. Most folks simply place the stone creature outside their home and make that the end of it.

However, if you want your gargoyle to be a magical creature of protection, you must bless it, name it, and welcome it into your home. How will you know its name? Sit with it, ask it, and listen. Once you know its name, never tell anyone! The name of your gargoyle is a best kept secret. You wouldn't want anyone to know its name, lest they call it and use it for their own purposes. (You can tell your family members the gargoyle's name, but only if they can keep a secret!)

Protecting Your Office Space

Many people work in offices or cube spaces they share with several people. Others are lucky enough to have their own office where they can close the door, thus creating a boundary between them and other people. Most workers, however, share their spaces with co-workers or work in close proximity with other people, where putting up a protective boundary can be difficult.

Sometimes you have to be sneaky with your protection. Here are a few simple ways to protect your office space.

Plants are a simple, easy way to add protective energy to an office space. Rosemary is a protective plant that most people associate with cooking. Adding a rosemary plant to your desk ushers in the protective energies of this ancient herb. As an added boost, slip a Mercury dime, a bit of graveyard dirt, or a protective crystal into the dirt. Arrange protective crystals such as smoky quartz or amethyst around the base of the plant. Cacti are also decorative and protective. Beautiful small cacti planted in small containers would sit nicely on one's desk.

Mirrors are superb tools of reflection and can be used to reflect negative energy. To use a mirror for protection, purchase a pocket-size mirror. Cleanse the mirror with Florida Water. Pass the mirror through the smoke of a sage bundle or the smoke from Palo Santo chips. Place the mirror in a spot where you can't look directly into it, but others will. This way, the mirror works as a deflective shield of harmful energy sent either directly or indirectly your way.

Many people keep photos of loved ones on their desks. There is nothing more calming than gazing into the faces of your friends, family, and loved ones while you're hard at work. But you can also use the frames that hold the photos of your loved ones as frames of protection.

Using the skills you learned in crafting protective mojos, create a protective petition paper, small enough to fit between the back of the photo and the picture frame. In your petition, include the name of your loved one and thank them for watching over you while you work.

When you have finished writing the petition and anointing it, instead of folding the paper into a packet, slip it into the frame so the words face you from behind the photo of your loved one. Shut the frame and anoint it with blessing oil such as frankincense essential oil, or a protective oil of your choice. Perform a smudging ritual upon the frame.

Once your frame has been anointed and blessed, set it in a conspicuous place on your desk or workstation. Only you will know the petition paper is enclosed in the frame while the smiling face of your beloved brings love and protection to your workday.

I Don't Work in an Office

What if you don't have a desk? Maybe your job entails you working at a counter or in a retail situation.

One of the most powerful symbols of protection is a five-pointed star, also known as a pentagram. In the second chapter, in the Lesser Banishing Ritual of the Pentagram, we discussed the significance of the pentagram and its power. Five-pointed stars are used as badges on people in authority. One look at that shiny star, and you know that person means business.

An easy way to protect yourself when you can't place an item in the open, is to draw a pentagram on the inside lining of your clothes. If you don't want the pentagram to be permanent, use chalk to draw a five-pointed star within a circle on the inside of your clothes. If you want the pentagram to be permanent, stitch one inside your clothes where it won't be seen and finish the magical act with a prayer of protection.

You can also smudge your clothing with white sage before wearing them. Give them a few minutes to air dry and the scent will be gone.

If you can wear jewelry, silver is a wonderful protective metal. If you can wear silver talismanic jewelry at your job, do so! Charge your silver jewelry by setting it out under the light of the full moon, saying prayers of protection over it, then wearing it on a daily basis or whenever you feel the need for extra protection.

be your own tree

HIGH ABOVE IN THE harsh windswept terrain of the Rocky Mountains stand ancient trees known as bristle cone pines. Their gnarly and twisted branches are a testament to their strength and voracity to withstand the elements and the ravages of time.

In the swamps of Louisiana and even in some graveyards stand gigantic cypress trees. Their bark has been revered as magical talismans for centuries. It is considered good juju to receive a piece of lightning-struck bark from a cypress tree. A piece of lightning-struck bark holds the power of the cataclysmic forces of thunder and electricity, forged into one powerful piece of elemental bark that can be used to bring about swift-as-lightning changes into one's life.

On Johns Island in North Carolina stands the Angel Oak Tree, a living oak whose very presence takes your breath away, whether you gaze upon it through the screen of your computer or are lucky enough to physically dance beneath its gigantic branches that sprawl above sacred soil. Local folk say the ghosts of slaves haunt the tree, as surely the tree was a witness to the atrocities of enslaved Africans as well as being a sacred place to heal their wounds.

I have wrapped my arms around the trunk of an old oak tree on the grounds of a plantation in Louisiana. I thanked it for being a witness and a testament to atrocities of slavery as well as being a place where my ancestors might have rested their weary bones under its shady branches.

And in Sedona, Arizona, stand the twisted spirals of vortex juniper trees, said to either aid you on your spiritual journey in a kind way, or turn you spiritually inside out, then back in again, as they feel is magically necessary for your spiritual growth. I speak from personal experience when I say some of those vortex trees in Sedona need signs that say, "Gaze upon me at your own risk!"

Not all trees make you want to cozy up to them or lounge beneath their shade-giving branches. Some trees have spikes and thorns. Some trees appear spooky when you look at them. Some trees have poisonous sap that will burn your skin.

Trees have been revered as magical beings since time immemorial, giving us wood to build our homes, paper to write upon, resins such as piñon and Palo Santo to burn for spiritual purposes, sacred mistletoe to kiss beneath, not to mention countless fruits, nuts, and berries to fill our bellies.

Scientifically speaking, trees are known as the lungs of the earth. Trees take in carbon dioxide and release oxygen. They inhale and exhale with us. To some, hugging a tree may seem as natural as hugging your best friend. Recent research shows trees may actually communicate through their elaborate roots systems, passing information necessary for survival from one tree to another. There may be a Mother Tree that cares for her baby trees by sending critical information through her underground root network.

Some trees such as aspens grow in magnificent groves, while others do well in orchards, such as apple, peach, and orange trees, to name a few. Trees are as varied and individual as you and me.

Spiritual Distinctions

In the world of the Craft, one may often hear groups referred to as covens or groves. The word *coven* is well known, but *grove* is less known. Traditionally, a coven is comprised of thirteen people, based on a hierarchy of a high priestess and/or priest, initiated members, and those seeking initiation. The coven may or may not confer degrees of Witchcraft.

A grove may function similarly to a coven, with a familiar hierarchy of a high priestess and/or a priest, but may follow a more loose structure where a group dynamic is cultured to allow members more of a say in how the group runs.

In Vodou, "houses" are composed of initiated members. A person must pass through initiation to become a member of a Vodou society. The leadership of the house flows from the Manbo, who is a female leader, or an Oungan, who is a male leader. Both are initiated, dedicated, and deeply devoted to the Lwa, and both have spent many years learning Vodou rituals, rites, and practices that allow the house to function. The body of the house is made up of members classified as Ounsi, Kanzo, and Laplas—each level being initiated and serving at a higher level to the Lwa and the house.

As you can see, the spiritual world has no shortage of structure or environments in which to flourish as you journey along your path. And lest we forget, many people also choose to remain solitary practitioners, as they may not feel called to work in groups, may feel intimidated in a group environment, or prefer the anonymity of a private practice.

Maintaining Your Magical Individuality

While many trees form in groves or exist together in tree societies, each tree must separately rise from the earth and reach its branches to the sky. Each tree must unfurl its leaves and take in water, which falls as rain, to grow and nourish its body. Each tree must stand on its own, while it remains part of the group of the living beings in the forest, the park, the urban jungle, or countryside. And when the wind blows hard, every tree must bend or break, while holding on to Mother Earth for strength, support, and sustenance.

As you set out to join with other magical people in groves, covens, houses, or communities, remember to be your own tree. It is good to take in nourishment, wisdom, and advice from those who have gone before you, but know it is also good to use discernment, listen to your gut, and heed your own spiritual guidance.

All trees have merit. All trees have value. Some trees are deciduous while others are evergreen. Some trees bloom magnificent perfumed blossoms while others have thorns.

Each tree is a living unique special being, rooted upon Mother Earth. Remember to stay rooted and grounded as you venture into the world of working for others, groups, and social media.

It is always good to be your own tree. If the ground you walk upon becomes unsteady or you lose your footing along the way, find a tree. Give it a hug and sit with it for awhile. Tell the tree your cares and woes, and before you know it, you'll feel refreshed, revived, and ready to carry on as you make your way through the world as a magical person.

▲▲▲▲▲▲▲▲▲▲▲▲▲▲▲▲▲▲▲▲▲▲▲▲▲

Spell to Communicate with a Tree

Items needed:

Your sincere desire to speak with the tree

A sincere offering such as flowers, a libation, or food

Find a tree that speaks to you. You will know this by the good feelings or emotions you experience when you pass or look upon the tree. Many earth-based people already have trees they revere as spiritual guides or friends.

Place your left hand on the trunk of the tree and your right hand on your heart. You are making a heart to heart connection with the tree. Speak to the tree sincerely either silently or vocally. It matters not what you say, but how you say it. The tree will understand and will receive your communication as long as you are respectful and sincere.

When your conversation is over, thank the tree and leave your offering. Know nature has heard you. Record in your magical journal any images or impressions you receive. Follow any hunches you receive. Consider donating or volunteering with an organization that cares for trees.

▼▼▼▼▼▼

Joining Groups

Many a magical soul ventures into the worlds of Hoodoo, folk magick, and Witchcraft with nary the intention of forming a community or joining a group. A solitary practice can feel safe. You never need disclose your thoughts or feelings to others. You never need to share your perspectives or experiences about your faith, practices, or path.

However, there is strength in numbers and venturing out to be with others of like mind can be a healing and rewarding experience. Finding your spot in a coven, grove, temple, house, or church (as some call their gatherings) allows you to meet and make new friends, explore new avenues of expression, and gain insight and knowledge previously unavailable to you as a solitary practitioner. As you grow in confidence and as you grow in relationship with your Higher Power or Deity, you may wish to seek out and meet up with folks who worship similarly.

Stepping into Vodou—A Personal Journey

I found myself in the position of wanting to be with like-minded people in the spring of 2017. My connection to the divine Marie Laveau had grown in love, strength, and power as I continued to work with her presence as a spiritual mentor, spiritual ancestor, and guide.

Following the guidance I received from my ongoing work with Marie Laveau, I attended my first St. John's Eve ritual ceremony and headwashing, which is held annually in New Orleans. Manbo Sallie Ann Glassman and the initiated members of La Source Ancienne Ounfo perform the ceremony and headwashing rite.

The headwashing ceremony can be used as a cleansing rite, purification, or as a step to Vodou initiation. It depends on the person and what they desire to achieve during the ceremony.

When we arrived in New Orleans, I was extremely nervous and excited. The city is a rich fertile bed of ghosts, spirits, and magick. The air was heavy with the promise of the night's ceremony.

Per Manbo Sallie Ann's public notice, participants had been instructed to wear all white clothing. Images of beautiful Black women dressed in white clothing, dancing around a fire, and performing ceremonies and rituals had long been in my periphery. It seemed they were always secretly whispering to me, but I was never ready to join them. One must honor one's guides and intuitions. One must listen to one's inner guidance and act accordingly.

Before I continue, I must take a moment and give a nod to my dear sweet husband, who accompanies me in all I do. He gives me his rock-solid support and stands by my side as my husband, companion, and friend. He was there with me during the headwashing ceremony and the ritual on Bayou St. John the following evening. He too was respectful of the attire and wore all-white clothing.

Night of the Headwashing Ceremony

When we arrived at the International House Hotel on the evening of June 22, 2017, preparations for the ritual and headwashing were underway. Many fine people all dressed in white were gathered together to see the unveiling of a new statue of Marie Laveau and participate in the evening's ritual.

Manbo Sallie Ann Glassman and members from La Source Ancienne Ounfo were also present, adding finishing touches to altars, while others were holding cornmeal in their hands, drawing vèvès. That evening marked my first time seeing vèvès drawn on the ground. A vèvè is a beautiful symbol drawn in cornmeal during a Vodou ceremony/ritual to call a particular Lwa.

Each Lwa (which is a Vodou Deity) has their own vèvè dedicated to them. As one progresses on the path of Vodou, one learns the vèvès associated with each Lwa and learns to draw them from memory.

Since attending my first Vodou ceremony, I have drawn vèvès using cornmeal and let me tell you, it is no easy task! As with all things that take time and effort to accomplish, those who are most capable at what they do make things appear easy. I have deep respect for the practitioners, Manbos, Oungans, and initiates of Vodou.

The ceremony was life changing. I found myself caught up in the rhythm of the drums, songs, prayers, and singing. As time neared to have our heads washed, I knew I was ready. I took my place in line and when it was my turn, I gratefully knelt on the floor, unwrapped the white scarf around my head, and let my long dreadlocks fall before Manbo Sallie Ann Glassman.

Time stopped or maybe it expanded. Whispers and prayers were said in my ear. Ancient voices spoke to me. Familiar and unfamiliar scents tickled my nose as cool water mixed with fragrant herbs was poured over my head.

When the headwashing was done, I was told to rewrap my head with the white scarf (thankfully, one of the beautiful ladies from La Source Ancienne Ounfo helped me with this task) and to keep my head wrapped all night, to remember the dreams or visions that came to me.

One of the most beautiful things about this ritual and the ceremony held on Bayou St. John the following evening is they are free and open to the public. Manbo Sallie Ann Glassman and the members of La Source Ancienne Ounfo remain tirelessly dedicated to the tradition of St. John's Eve and the legacy of Marie Laveau.

True Immersion and the Benefits of Joining Groups

A year later, in the spring of 2018, I returned to New Orleans and was formally initiated into La Source Ancienne Ounfo. My initiation into Vodou has been a magnificent and wondrous enhancement to my spiritual life and soul.

While going all the way to formal initiation may not be your cup of tea when you first set out on your magical path, as you continue to journey along, I do recommend seeking out groups and/or festivals and events where you can join with others who practice and worship similarly. As you can imagine, practicing paths or faiths not of the mainstream can be a lonely and isolating experience. One needs to touch base with other humans swimming in the waters of spirituality to grow, learn, heal, and celebrate life.

A word of caution: Not all groups and communities are created similarly. The worlds of the occult and spirituality are no different than the mundane world when it comes to organizations created and run by people.

Many a newbie or dedicated seeker has had their heart broken, feelings hurt, or confidences betrayed by those who appear to be of value and integrity in positions of leadership. My story of initiation into Vodou took many years of seeking and trying, failing and succeeding at finding the right group for *me*.

When you first set out to join with groups, do some research on the people you feel drawn to. Ask around, search the internet, and see if there are public events you can attend as a silent observer so you can observe the group's dynamics and interactions with others, without anyone knowing you may be considering joining.

And by all means, once you do join the group, if things start to smell foul or you're not receiving what you need to help you continue to grow on your spiritual path, in accordance with your highest good, get out. There is no shame in deciding a group or community isn't working for you.

Always remember no one owns this knowledge. It is given to us by the soul of the universe for our enlightenment, growth, and development. As we knock upon the doors of spirit, some doors will open, others may stay shut. Some doors allow you a glimpse inside, while others completely open to you.

Try not to get discouraged if a door you knock upon turns out to be a sh*t hole. Once your wounds have healed from disillusionment and disappointment, you'll be a stronger spiritual person, ready to carry on your spiritual journey.

Resources for Finding Groups

Fortunately in this day and age, the internet has brought the opportunity to meet with others right to your fingertips. A search of "Pagan festivals near me" will return a plethora of options for meets and greets with your people. If you physically can't make it to an event or need to take baby steps before joining up with a group, YouTube is wonderful, as well as Facebook, for creating virtual connections with like-minded people who share your aspirations and intentions for spiritual gathering.

Prayer for Joining Groups

Dear [insert name of your Higher Power or Deity],
I, [insert your name], *desire to connect with like-
minded people who share my values, sincerity, and
desire for community. Thank you for watching over
me, blessing me, and keeping me as I journey into
new adventures that bring me closer to you. I know
I am always guided and protected. I thank you for
your blessings upon my spirit, my journey, my
goals, my dreams, and my desires. Blessed be.*

Social Media

We live in unprecedented times. We are among the first people
to live with the invention of Facebook, Twitter, Instagram, Snap-
chat, and YouTube, websites and applications that connect us to
the virtual universe of humanity, with just the touch of a finger.

With this unprecedented access comes the ability to share our
lives, stories, successes, and failures. We can cheer each other on
and support each other during tough times. We can ride the roll-
ercoaster of life together, laugh with each other, cry, and grieve
with each other. We can look at countless photos of cats and dogs,
selfies, and pictures of our loved ones as we celebrate and navigate the mountains and valleys of life.

But for all the good the internet and its unfathomable bastion
of websites have brought us, dark things have come too. There is
the dark web, fake news, and false ideas that appear real. Strangers can peer into things considered private. A person can have
their financial information hacked and stolen, and people can
be bullied from sources that can never be traced. "Bots" can troll
accounts, and software viruses can spread like wildfire, just by

opening an email you thought was personally addressed to you. Huge data breaches have occurred from trusted sources leaving people feeling vulnerable and exposed. Ads track us from site to site, trying to sell us things they think we need but don't want.

But we can't turn the internet or social media off. This is the way of the world. Digital media and technology are here to stay. No matter if you think you're not "online," or an online person, if you use the internet or your cell phone for banking, email, or uploading photos, or sending data to the cloud, you're online.

And while I do see value in using the internet and social media to connect with people of like-minded paths, I would feel unscrupulous if I didn't drop a word of caution about opening up your entire magical life online, especially if you are new or a beginner.

For as large and vast as the internet may be, the magical world is still very small. As you near people at the top, the circle becomes smaller and smaller. It may seem as if we live in an endless global magical community, but in reality it's a small group of dedicated folks who have persisted in keeping the ways of Divine Mystery open to the public.

A hint to the wise is sufficient, for even though we strive to live lives of integrity, people make mistakes. Even the best of us have flaws. Disappointments and hurt feelings can and will occur. And nothing travels faster than gossip in an online community. Rumors and jealousy can do serious harm to a person's life.

Guidelines for Social Media Etiquette

If you belong to online groups and societies, I implore you at some point to do the following:

Actually meet the people you converse with, either by attending a festival or local community event. You may be surprised to learn the people you deeply trust online can be night-and-day different in person. On the other hand, you may be pleasantly surprised to learn you're dealing with the real thing when you meet your online buddy in person.

Search your own name from time to time. We all leave trails when we go online. It's a good idea to check every now and then what the web attaches to your name. Everybody does a people search on new people they meet. Be proactive in what the internet shares about you. If you see discrepancies, contact the website owner to have erroneous information corrected or deleted.

Should conflict arise, which often happens in groups, never bash people publicly in online forums. You would be amazed how easily anger, rage, and harsh words can spread and may eventually damage your reputation.

Even if you are a member of a "closed" group, know that nothing is ever truly deleted or secure. (I speak from experience as a person with a background in information technology.) If you're prepared to type it online, know it may be breeched or shared. Your best defense is transparency! Keep it clean, keep it honest, and keep it sincere. If you truly need to vent or discuss relationships gone sideways, do it in person or over the phone.

If you need to discuss things of a sensitive nature via email, for heaven's sake never "reply all" on emails you're sending that contain sensitive information. Another good check is to type your email and send it to yourself before you send it to the group or an individual. That way, you can truly see firsthand how it ends up in the mailbox. And if you're really paranoid, you can always "bcc" (blind carbon copy) yourself and people you trust, so you and your trusted confidants receive a copy of the email. The recipient never sees the people in the "bcc" subject line, and you have a digital copy of the email you sent.

Always remember your online persona is a representation of you and your community. Aspire to be a role model and an example. Honor those who have come before you, or to the ones who will come after you, by taking time to think over your words before you post them. For we all stand on the shoulders of those who have come before us. Many people made sacrifices, shouldered ill will and persecution so we could be here today, with the ability to be "out of the broom closet," living openly as we see fit. Let us honor our gifts by using them for the highest good.

Protect your computer space and environment. Place protective and good energy crystals near your computer. Keep fresh flowers on your desk. Light a candle when you work. Burn incense or sage when you sit down to compose an email. Cleanse your workspace on a daily basis with Florida Water. Put happy images on your desktop. All these things will help to keep the good juju flowing as you venture out into the worlds of virtual reality.

And lastly, take a break from the world of social media from time to time. Give yourself permission not to check your email, log onto Facebook, post a Tweet, or upload photos to Instagram for an afternoon or an entire day. As much as we benefit from being socially connected, it can also rob us of our thoughts, feelings, and our own intuitive connections.

Many magical people are highly empathic people (meaning we are able to feel deep emotions and take on feelings of others). We can become easily overwhelmed by the constant barrage of posts—good and bad, horror stories of life as the news sees fit to spin it, and the seamless jump from someone's successes to the passing of a friend's loved one, all with the scroll of a finger.

As you navigate and make connections through social media, remember it's good to take a break from it too. Your mind, body, and spirit will thank you. And when you return to virtual reality, you'll be refreshed and ready to reconnect.

move your body—
revive your spirit

IN ONE OF MY all-time favorite films, *On a Clear Day You Can See Forever*, Barbra Streisand's character, Daisy Gamble, enters into hypnosis to stop smoking and discovers wondrous things about her life. As Daisy continues her hypnotherapy, fascinating past life memories begin to surface. Needless to say, Daisy is forever changed by her experiences.

Have you ever gazed into a soap bubble? Have you ever held it on the tip of your finger, watching the colors swirl around, and felt yourself fall into worlds only glimpsed by a child?

Have you ever stood beside the ocean or a lake and watched the moon light a path across the water just for you?

It's our childlike sense of wonder and awe that propels us into magical places and experiences. Sadly, as we get older, the world pounds away at us and tells us over and over to let go of our childlike sense of wonder, that to be an adult we must put away our childish things. Rubbish. It's all rubbish.

I would venture to say one of the reasons you're reading this book is because you're one of those people for whom childlike things, like secrets and wishes, and believing in enchanted places, have never been far from your heart. You've embraced the light upon a stone, portals opening that you can't see with your naked eye, but know they exist within the truth in your soul. You've heard the whispers of spirit in the dark, seen the universe unfold in a shooting star, and felt the magick in the fading light of the setting sun.

It's not our fault when we lose our sense of wonder. Life can be hard, relentless, and pounding. It can disappoint us and break our hearts. It can tell us over and over again, there's no reason to be this way, to believe in magick, spells, and potions. It can tell us there is no need to keep practicing a belief, a faith, in which you're a minority or most people think you're slightly crazy for doing so.

But haven't all the great ones fallen under the exact same ridicule? Didn't many artists and creatives spend their entire lives working and creating pieces that so many didn't understand or even appreciate until they were gone?

Lift your eyes and look to the skies. Watch a flock of geese fly across the sky or hear a crow release the first caw of the day, and you'll know in your heart you're on the right path. Listen to the ocean waves break upon the shore and feel the chill of the rhythms of the universe run up and down your spine. Nature is always whispering to us, beckoning us to believe.

As earth-based magical people, we need to get up and go outside, gaze into soap bubbles, or listen to calming ethereal music to fuel our souls. Yes, it is good to read and gather knowledge, but it is also tantamount to our spiritual growth to get up and get physical. A physical practice is important for grounding and centering, as well as maintaining our magical balance in the world. It's easy to get drawn into heady practices and neglect the benefits of moving bodies. A practice that gets your body moving complements your spiritual practices. One should always strive to maintain balance within our minds, bodies, and spirit.

Go for a Walk

When I started writing this chapter, I was recovering from foot surgery. Taking my daily walk with my dog had ceased to be an event I looked forward to and enjoyed. My foot was off balance and it was difficult to walk very far without discomfort or sometimes pain. But slowly, bit-by-bit, I managed. One day at a time, one step at a time, after procuring one copious wide shoe after another, I was able to get outside and go for a walk with my sweet dog.

I needed to go for a walk as much as I needed to drink water and eat food. I needed to walk as much as I needed to stand under the moon and stars. I needed to walk to refresh and replenish my soul, my magical self and being.

When I walk I don't plug my ears with headphones. Walking is a spiritual boost for the mind, body, and spirit. The good thing about walking is almost anyone can do it. Walking meets you where you are, whether you can click along at a fast pace or gingerly take just a step or two at a time because you're recovering from an illness, have chronic pain, or need the assistance of a caregiver.

I'm an urban Witch. My view consists of city neighborhoods, alleyways, and streets. And yet, when I get outside for a walk, I'm able to take in the sights and blessings from trees, squirrels, dogs, cats, clouds, people, and landscapes.

Many who practice the Craft of the old ways are city dwellers. It can be a chore for us to find serenity in the city. Yet if we can muster the energy of taking one small step at a time, by getting outside and taking a walk, nature will unfold for us in a myriad of ways we may not have ever imagined. And if you're a country dweller, the same holds true, although I suspect country dwellers have more opportunities at their front door for experiencing the magick of nature, without having to travel far for peace, quiet, and serenity.

And let's face it. Many magical people live in their heads. We think about everything! A lot of us are empathic, clairsentient, or clairvoyant. We feel things *deeply,* which means we need the soothing comfort of nature perhaps more than most.

When you get outside for a bit, without your headphones on, it's a chance for your other senses to take over. Your feet become your roots and your guides. Your hearing guides you to one street or another and your eyes see things only a magical person can see.

Taking a walk boosts your magical prowess. As you saunter down sidewalks or country roads, relaxing into your pace, your mind slows down and opens to input from spirit. You never know what you might pick up in terms of magick as you take a moment to go outside.

You never know who you might meet as you're walking or what you may find. You may be amazed at the relationships you build with people who get to know you, simply from your presence as you walk by their yard or doorstep. And it's a good thing for magical people to get out and mingle with the rest of the world. We don't have to go around wearing *Witch, priestess,* or *conjurer* on our sleeves. Our good natures and positive energies will speak for us as we pass by others, taking in the sights and sounds of urban neighborhoods and country landscapes. So by all means, to stay connected and rooted, open and receiving, get outside and take a walk!

Kung Fu and T'ai Chi

Years ago, I stood perusing the shelves of my favorite used bookstore. As I gleefully stared at the plethora of metaphysical and spiritual titles just waiting to be read, my hands landed on a book titled *A Grimoire of Shadows*, written by Ed Fitch, one of the pioneer authors on Witchcraft.

The pages of this book were yellowed with age, but the wisdom and knowledge I gained remain relevant to this day. One particular passage made a deep impression upon my mind. It was three paragraphs about the study of self-defense. The first two sentences called deeply to my mind, body, and spirit:

> *The world is not a peaceful or tranquil place, and it is seldom prudent to fully trust outsiders—even those appointed by the Law—with the safety of oneself, one's family, or those of one's coven. All should be encouraged to take some training in Karate, Hapkido, Judo, Ninjutsu, Aikido, T'ai Chi, Kung Fu, or other such martial arts which have a strong (if subtle) metaphysical and magical philosophy behind them.*

I found this to be correct. Studying martial arts does bring an added confidence and skill to the magical practitioner. Training in martial arts helps one focus, direct intentions, slow down and breathe, and build confidence.

Breathe In—Breathe Out/T'ai Chi

One aspect of Chinese martial arts that is commonly associated with focusing, grounding, and centering is T'ai Chi.

Although T'ai Ch'i is taught by many as a "meditation in motion," T'ai Chi Ch'uan as it is properly called in Kung Fu, means *grand ultimate fist* and is a fierce internal form of Kung Fu. Many people enjoy long years of health and longevity by practicing T'ai Chi as a meditative art, without ever studying T'ai Chi as a form of self-defense.

T'ai Chi and Chi Kung, both internal martial art forms in the lineage of Kung Fu, build strength, stamina, and focus by building one's Qi (pronounced *chee*) slowly and deliberately over time. Your Qi is your internal energy that resonates from your core or, if you have studied chakras, from your root chakra to your crown chakra. All your power stems from having strong Qi, a core of energy that you can use and draw from as a magical person.

I began studying T'ai Chi and Kung Fu at the ripe old age of 49, in the year of 2009! One is never too old to begin. If you have a desire to change and grow, life will always bring opportunities and avenues to meet your goals.

In June 2016, I achieved the rank of second-degree black belt under the tutelage and training of my Kung Fu Masters, David and Sharon Soard, who keep the art of Kung Fu and T'ai Chi alive in our school, the Chinese Shao-lin Center in Denver, Colorado.

It is with their blessing and permission I share the following daily exercise (written in my own words) that does wonders to keep your body healthy, your spirit vibrant, and your Qi strong. One of the best things about Kung Fu and T'ai Chi is you can do the exercises anywhere, any place and at any time. One does not need excessive amounts of equipment or specific outfits or clothing to wear. All you need is time and a space in which to move your body.

Ch'uan Breathing

Learning how to breathe, relax, ground, and center can do wonders for your health and longevity. This exercise is a good way to gently touch the benefits of Kung Fu and T'ai Chi. In between each step, take time to pause briefly.

To begin:

1. Stand with your feet firmly planted on the ground, shoulder's width apart and your arms hanging vertically by your side.

2. Raise your arms so they are parallel to the ground and extend horizontally in front of you. Your palms should be open and facing the ground, with your fingers pointing forward.

3. Turn your hands over and make two fists. Your fists will be facing upwards.

4. Inhale through your nose and pull your fists toward you.

5. Exhale through your mouth as you turn your fists downward, and extend your arms forward again. Your arms and fists will be parallel with the ground.

6. Open your hands. Turn your hands so your palms are facing upward.

7. Inhale through your nose and pull your palms toward you.

8. Exhale through your mouth and return your arms so they are hanging vertically at your sides. This concludes Ch'uan breathing.

Next, relax your neck and shoulders. And again, take time to pause briefly in between each step.

1. Tuck your chin to your chest.

2. Gently roll your head (don't force the movement) to the left, making a complete circle back to the starting position.

3. Gently roll your head to the right, making a complete circle back to the starting position. Lift your chin and return your head to its normal position.

4. Gently roll your shoulders forward, then backward.

5. Gently swing your arms from side to side, as you touch your left shoulder with your right hand, and touch your right shoulder with your left hand. Repeat this movement three to four times.

6. End the exercise by repeating steps one through eight for Ch'uan breathing.

To further your studies of T'ai Chi and Kung Fu, add the book *There Are No Secrets: Professor Cheng Man-ch'ing and His T'ai Chi Chuan* by Wolfe Lowenthal to your magical library. This book contains delightful photos, stories, and exercises that will help alleviate stress and bless you with health and longevity.

Terra Firma

Terra firma is our Mother Earth on whom we live, move, and have our being. She is the sustenance of all things, the giver of life, the receiver of death, and the soil from which new life springs eternal.

As magical people, many of us tend to be earth-centric folks. We live our lives in tune with the phases of the moon, the rising of the sun, and the turn of the Wheel. We are innately tuned to the first blades of grass in the spring, the golden leaves of autumn, and the first snowfall of winter. And while we perform rituals, rites, and spells in accordance with these changes, we also need moments, spaces of time where doing mundane tasks, such as sweeping our steps, pulling weeds, taking out the trash, and turning soil in gardens, keeps our physical bodies grounded and centered, and firmly planted on the earth.

It's easy as a magically spiritual person to get your head lost in the clouds. While we look to the sky for messages from spirit, we also need to get physical and keep our relationship with Mother Earth solid.

The tasks that follow don't require spells or rituals. All that is needed is your willingness to get down and dirty and enjoy the fulfillment from a job well done, and to keep your feet planted firmly on the earth and your heart connected to spirit.

Spring Cleanup

After the long sleep of winter, the earth gives her first nod of awakening by sending tender shoots of green grass through her dark soil. This is a fabulous time to dust off your rakes, find your broom, and grab your gardening gloves and trash bags to use as hardy friends to help you clean up your yard, your sidewalk, or your garden.

Begin by embracing the scent of fresh air on a spring day. Take a moment to breathe in the aroma of new life, readying itself to burst forth. If you have a yard, get outside and clean it up. You don't have to feel pressured to do it all in one day. Sometimes great satisfaction can be found in doing little bits at a time.

As you rake old soil and clean up leaves left over from the fall and winter seasons, notice the stirrings and thoughts that occur in your mind, body, and spirit. You may begin to daydream about what you'll plant and harvest later in the year. These daydreams may be about plants, flowers, and herbs for your garden, or they could be goals, dreams, wishes, and desires you'd like to manifest into reality.

Sweep your home. If you're so inclined, buy a new broom for the special occasion, sprinkle it with water, then sweep your home from the back of the house to the front door. When you're done, pour yourself a cup or glass of your favorite libation and enjoy the moment of having freshly swept floors. If you live where you have steps or a sidewalk outside, be sure to sweep that too. In time, sweeping or cleaning your steps, which is a mundane task, may be one that brings you contentment and satisfaction.

Clean Out Your Closets

A closet is a portal to dimensions of what to wear, old things you don't want to wear, or stuff you stick in there because you don't know what to do with it.

Cleaning out your closet frees up space in your home and in your mind. At least once a year, make a firm decision to clean out a closet. If the closet holds clothes, notice which clothes you haven't worn in a year, put them in a bag, and donate them. Many businesses will happily take your used clothing. The point is to get old things out of your home to make room for the new.

If your closet is stuffed with boxes and trinkets you haven't looked at in years, or you've decided to clean out your garage, take a deep breath and dig in! Open those dusty boxes and decide what is necessary to keep and what can move on. You can donate things other than clothes to resale shops and secondhand stores, or have a garage sale to release and let go of things that no longer serve you.

Flowers, Plants, and Herbs

Many who walk the path of magical spirituality are natural gardeners. They instinctively know when to turn the soil and pore over catalogs and websites filled with new plants and flowers to grow. They love getting their hands dirty as they tend their gardens. For others, nothing could be further from the truth. Some have no desire to pull up weeds from an overgrown plot, and the thought of bringing a live plant into their home fills them with dread. Others simply have lives too busy to care for a living plant.

Not to worry! If you're a natural gardener, get outside and enjoy turning your soil, taking trips to the local garden store or nursery, planting in the spring, watering and pruning through the summer, and harvesting in the fall season. Have fun planting your herbs, vegetables, and flowers. Hang potted plants outside your home or create your own. But be careful, it's easy to go overboard with purchasing plants when the nurseries first open!

If gardening isn't your thing, a trip to your local grocery store or nursery can supply you with fresh and inexpensive flowers and herbs to place on your altar. One doesn't need to break the bank purchasing flowers, plants, and herbs in order to connect with nature. If you choose to purchase fresh-cut flowers, just be sure to replace them with new ones once the blossoms have faded. If you'd like to try your hand at fresh herbs, choose a bright sunny place, such as a windowsill in your kitchen, or a room that gets southern exposure, so your herbs will receive lots of beautiful sunlight. Also, be sure to place a saucer underneath your potted herbs to prevent any overflow of water mishaps!

Terra firma is our mother and our friend. She provides all we need to live long and prosper. All she asks is that we remember her, celebrate her, and honor the gifts she so freely gives us.

Dance, Drum, and Sing

Shake the pillars of heaven. Sweat until you can't breathe, spin and turn, stomp your feet. Move your hips, shimmy across the floor, and clap your hands. The drum is calling you!

The drum is the heartbeat of the universe. Its rhythm connects us to the soul of the ancients and ones who have gone before us. Its pulse drives our emotions and fuels the movements of our bodies. The drum communicates our intentions and connects us to spirit. We are living drums, pulsating and gyrating to the syncopated movements of the cosmos.

Many cultures groove to the rhythm of the drum. All across the world, the drum can be found as an instrument of celebration, ritual, and ceremony.

In Japan, Taiko drummers beat their enormous drums with batons. Celtic drummers play hard beats on bodhráns and snare drums. Indian drummers play tablas, a set of two drums that produce an open, haunting sound. They are often accompanied by the rhythm of the mridangam drum, which answers and responds to the sound of the tabla. Listen to Hindu music and the sound of the mridangam drum, which lies on its side, is easily recognizable, and is familiar to the ear.

In Haiti, master drummers play tanbous and talking drums, pounding out beats so fast one can hardly keep up with their pace. They play spiritual music in honor of Vodou traditions that fire up your soul and bring your spirit into communication with the Lwa. In the New Orleans Vodou ceremonies I've attended, the master Haitian drummers drive your spirit into ecstasy and send your soul flying beyond the physical realms of time and space. Many people find themselves trancing out or writhing on the ground communicating with the Lwa. You may never be the same once you return to the boundaries of physical earth after dancing in a sacred Vodou ceremony!

In New Orleans, in a sacred place called Congo Square, enslaved Africans were allowed to gather and dance to the beat of their homeland on Sundays. The African people brought drums and rhythms that eventually became the foundations of jazz. They brought instruments that were the forerunners of the banjo and handheld percussive instruments.

Sundays in Congo Square during the time of slavery were a sacred and holy time. It was only on this day enslaved Africans could be free to dance and express themselves wholeheartedly to the beats of their homeland. To this day, Congo Square remains an honored and sacred place where people of all races and ethnicities gather to dance, harmonize, picnic, and socialize.

Another proud tradition of drumming and singing is honored in the Native American culture of the powwow. Denver, Colorado, and Albuquerque, New Mexico, host two of the largest powwows on the North American continent. At powwows, Native American nations from all over North America gather to dance and compete in a spectacular display of sacred regalia to the beat of gigantic drums, sometimes referred to as mother drums, that set your pulse on fire.

As magical people, if you live in North America, I encourage you to attend a powwow at least once in your life. If your travels ever take you to New Orleans, stop by Congo Square and pay homage to the ancestors of enslaved Africans, to whom we owe a great debt of gratitude for their sacrifices and contributions to music. So powerful was the heartbeat of the drum that Africans used them as a form of communication; and when there was no drum to beat on, enslaved Africans used whatever they could find to take the place of it. In many major U.S. cities, it is not uncommon to see young men using plastic buckets as drums, playing incredible music for locals, hoping someone will drop a few coins or dollars in their hat.

The musical genres of jazz, rock and roll, hip-hop, and the ever-influential rhythm and blues all owe their start to African beats. It is easy to trace their musical legacies to the Crescent City of New Orleans and the winding waters of the Mississippi River. One can easily hear jazz, rock and roll, R&B, and combinations of new sounds emanating from clubs and dance halls in the French Quarter on any given day, night, or Sunday afternoon.

Many Pagan communities also hold drum circles. Spiritually earth-based people love to get together and drum, dance, and sing. It is hard to beat a night of drumming by a roaring fire, with the full moon shining overhead, in a secluded grove or park, with thirty or so of your closest Pagan friends. With the invention of social media, one can easily search "drum circles near me" and find a group for a night of drumming and dancing. The website Witchvox.com is a fantastic resource for locating Pagan events, rituals, and ceremonies open to the public, arranged on a state-by-state basis.

And if drumming and singing in a large group of people just isn't your thing, you can always pound out your rhythms in the private sanctuary of your own backyard or home. There have been many a night where it has just been me and my drum, my own heartbeat, and the moon, dancing in harmony to the music of the season.

One also needn't spend a tremendous amount of money acquiring their first drum. Used drums can be found for sale online, at garage sales, and in secondhand stores.

YouTube is also a fantastic source for watching videos of people drumming all across the world, singing songs, and dancing. You may even pick up a song or two to add to your repertoire.

Allow yourself the freedom to express your gratitude for living, your connection to the ancient ones, and your joyous nature for being an expression of the Divine Mysteries by drumming, dancing and singing. Who knows? You just might be the creator of a new dance or rhythm we all can groove to.

ligHteN up

WHEW! EVEN THOUGH IN the last chapter you read about ways to move your body and revive your spirit, you've also been through some heavy magick. We began our journey by learning rituals, how to cleanse our spaces, do spell work, practice Hoodoo, and discover ways to connect with our Higher Power.

We also learned how to work with altars, craft mojos, step into the crossroads, work in the graveyard, and the importance of maintaining your spiritual individuality. That is a lot of spiritual direction and guidance!

Even though all the above are important in your life as a magical practitioner, it is equally important to lighten up, laugh at yourself, and give yourself a break. Even the most magical people among us need to go to the movies or a concert, hang out with friends, be with their family, turn off their cell phones, step away from the computer, quell the desire to post on social media, or take an old-fashioned vacation every once in a while.

Sometimes, and especially when we're new on our magical spiritual paths, we tend to consume every book, tome, or grimoire and spend all our time studying and practicing. That is completely understandable because learning magick and discovering your spirituality is fun, exciting, and powerful too. But if you don't take a break once in a while it can become easy not to see the forest for all the magical trees!

Many people who find themselves drawn to these ways are "heady" people, considered good students, dog-with-a-bone people, who will succeed at all costs. While these are good traits for success, one can easily become overwhelmed, frustrated, or disappointed when outcomes don't manifest as one had originally intended.

That's why every spell worker needs to take a break. You can burn yourself out quickly by obsessing over spell work and whether you have the right materials, did you start it at the right time, is the moon in the right position, and so on and so on.

You can tire yourself out by attending too many festivals or rituals and signing up for every class your local metaphysical shop offers. You can also do yourself a disservice by getting too many readings or carting home every crystal that catches your eye. Believe me, I speak from experience!

Not to mention your family, friends, and loved ones, as well as your fur babies may begin to feel neglected if you don't take a break or lighten up! You may also find yourself having magical tunnel vision, if you don't get out once in a while and smell the roses and gaze at the sky. There comes a time when one must step away from the magick and reengage with life, simply as a human being. In today's society, we're all encouraged to do more, be more, constantly compete with others who we think are beating us to the prize. But the prize of the work you do is the greater power within yourself, so there is no competition.

More importantly, by stepping away and doing mundane tasks, such as your laundry, yardwork, or cooking dinner, you may find that insights or perspectives come to you, which may be just the answer you were looking for while you were intensely pouring over your magical books. A multitude of benefits come by having a good laugh or just sitting in the park. And many of us hardcore folks have also learned that if you don't take time to lighten up and relax, the universe may do it for you by sending you "blessings" that force you to step away for awhile from your magical studies.

As you go forth into the sections of the chapter, put your feet up, exhale, and give yourself a break. You've earned a spiritual timeout. You have my permission not to comb your hair for a day, stay in your pajamas, binge-watch your favorite TV shows or movies, color in your coloring books, be with your family, take Fido for a walk, or pet Princess Fiona until she purrs. Get a massage, if you like that sort of thing, make an appointment at a fabulous salon, get your hair done, or schedule yourself for a well-deserved mani-pedi. You could even chuck all your magical studies for awhile and pick up your hammer and saw and build something crafty or turn on your hot glue gun and make something fun out of all your leftover magical whatnots and thing-a-ma-jigs.

It's up to you. You decide what timeout present suits yourself best. Your magick will always be there for you, waiting to be picked up, just where you left it. So don't worry, taking a magical break is well worth it!

Belly Laughs and Magical Blunders

Congratulations! You've learned how to do powerful rites and rituals, craft mojos, and work with altars.

But lest we get ahead of ourselves, it's good to remember that even the most Witchy, powerful, and practiced of us makes mistakes and flubs up every once in a while. All seriousness aside, magick is supposed to be fun. If you lose your childlike sense of wonder and awe while practicing magick, you are shortchanging yourself!

Your inner child loves to laugh and play. Which of us doesn't still marvel at floating soap bubbles or become giddy with delight when staring at shelves filled with oils, lotions, and potions? Let's face it, many of us got on the magick train from platforms filled with childhood dreams of Witches in pointy hats, bubbling cauldrons, dusty old magical books, and movies loaded with flying monkeys, and even a snitch or two!

So before you get to thinking you have to be perfect in every spell or ritual you perform, here are some anecdotes to help lighten your load. I hope these tidbits will be of help to you, if you ever consider giving up your magical path because your stuff just doesn't seem to come out right!

Always Remember: Never Put a Smoking Cauldron Near a Fire Alarm

One of the great things about working magick is that we do it in secret. We tap into spirit, align with our guides, say our prayers, and get to workin'. Most often we get up early to perform our magical acts or we do them late at night around the Witching hour when most people are fast asleep or settling into dream land.

But what happens when you've got yourself ready and prepared all your necessary items for your work, and then you set off the house fire alarm because you put a smoking cauldron near the sensor? Of course your intention was to cleanse your home of negativity. But however well-intentioned your work, you instead succeeded at waking your husband out of a deep sleep at o'dark thirty in the morning, and he isn't too thrilled to see and smell smoke and incense filling up the house.

You humble yourself profusely and keep going! Yes indeed. You will find more often than not, when you enter into serious spell work or paths of initiation, that all sorts of blunders and obstacles show up to test your commitment. So if you find yourself with alarms blaring and people wondering what the hell you are doing at that hour of the morning or night, stop, apologize, and when everything settles down, keep going and get right back to your spell work.

Sometimes the lesson is not that your spell work is awesome, it's that you have the tenacity to keep going!

You're having a trusted and confidential meeting with a magical mentor, only to discern your skirt is stuck in your panties, and everyone has seen your underwear!

Yes, this happened to me. We all have people we look up to in our magical communities and getting a face-to-face meeting with them in this age of texting and internet chatting is a downright momentous and special occasion. So prior to your face-to-face meeting, you do your best to look good and be prepared, but during the meeting as all humans must do, you need to go to the bathroom.

You make it to the bathroom and back to your table with no hiccups. You didn't trip or bump into someone's table while maintaining your calm, suave, magical demeanor. But just as you sit down, a kind, elderly white-haired lady makes her way to your table, her eyes intent on your face, ready to whisper something only you can hear.

You lean forward. You're just sure she is there to whisper a message from spirit but instead she says, "Honey, your skirt is hiked up in your underwear!"

Mortified and embarrassed, your face blushes and you thank the kind lady for her magical message. You stand, untuck your skirt and sit back down, while your magical friend has a good belly laugh, and you do too.

Lesson: check your backside before you leave the bathroom to make sure your magical underwear isn't showing!

You're wearing the wrong clothes to ritual

You've read the invitation over and over. You've highlighted and packed everything you need for your magical ritual experience. You've got all the necessary items, including having your hair just right, comfy shoes for standing all night, as well your phone charged and set to silent.

You pull up to the designated location. As other participants disembark from their cars, you quickly realize you're wearing the wrong colors! You thought you were supposed to be wearing all white, but everyone is wearing all black!

Your solution? Underneath all your white clothes you are wearing black leggings and a black camisole, because everyone knows if you wear black undergarments under white clothes, you can't see the fleshy parts or your underwear. So quickly you strip off your white clothes, and head to the ritual wearing the appropriate black color.

Lesson: always wear or bring a second layer of clothing to rituals you're not familiar with, so if you need to change, you can do it quickly and no one will be the wiser.

You're teaching a class at a Pagan retreat when you suddenly realize more than half of the participants are embracing the choice to go skyclad (naked), and you're fully dressed in your professional Witchy teaching clothes.

We've all been told if you get nervous as a public speaker, just imagine your audience naked. Well, this experience takes it to a new level!

As you become more experienced and practiced as a magical person or practitioner, people may indeed seek you out for speaking engagements or as a teacher in your local community.

Lesson: if you're the teacher and you're fully dressed and most of your audience is not, keep your eyes forward!

Never wear a dead man's shoes to a Halloween all-night walkathon.

A dear friend of mine is a sharp dresser. He's a well-put-together magical man who appreciates style and class. However, during a celebration of Halloween far from home he found himself without the proper shoes to wear.

Being a savvy shopper, he popped into a swanky second-hand store. Immediately, he was drawn to a pair of red shoes he couldn't live without. He promptly paid for his shoes, added them to his wardrobe for the evening, and strutted around looking fine and handsome.

But as the hours began to take their toll on his feet, it became painfully apparent his "new" shoes were not a fit. They pinched his feet and turned his usual pleasant and friendly disposition into one that others would be well advised to stay away from.

Lesson: always bring a second set of magical shoes to wear when traveling. A dead man's shoes can definitely tell tales.

Take Your Time

Stepping your toes into the waters of the occult, Hoodoo, and folk magick can be an exhilarating, thrilling, and sometimes even a scary experience. At one moment you can be sure of your footing, while the next moment you may feel as if you're being carried downstream by a force not of your own power.

These feelings can be intense and powerful, or downright frightening, especially when one is new to the magical path. Tapping into your intuitive core, fueled with the knowledge you've gained, and the exhilaration that comes from working magick, can sometimes throw a person off balance. Which is why I recommend after doing particularly powerful spell work, you take a moment to ground and center, breathe and relax.

Below are some ways you can incorporate grounding and centering after doing spell work:

- Change your clothes. Wash whatever you wore during your spell work. If possible after washing your clothes, hang them outside and let the element of air refresh your garments.
- Take a bath or a shower. Use your favorite soap or shower gel, take your time and enjoy a luxurious bath. You've earned it.

- Put on fresh clean clothes. This signals to your brain and your spirit that spell-work time is over.

- Eat some nourishing food. Eating after ritual is a common practice among many practitioners. Eating grounds your body to the earth and refuels your spirit.

- Drink some water. Water is life. Every living thing on Earth needs water. After you've been working in the realm of magick, it's easy to be dehydrated. Drinking water is a wonderful way to return your mind, body, and spirit to the realm of everyday living. For even as we are magical people, we're still humans, and human beings need water.

- Take a moment to sit and collect your thoughts about your experiences with an ice cold drink, a hot cup of tea, a glass of wine or even a cocktail, once you've properly hydrated your body. Take time to review how things are going.

For even though you've set upon your magical path with good intentions, sometimes the path twists and turns, and it can be easy to lose your way. Also, when we find a fit with knowledge we've been seeking, we tend to go as fast as we can, impervious to nudges to slow down, then we suddenly want to hang up our shingle and start putting everything we've learned into practice.

There is a reason why the Hermit in the tarot is an old man or woman. There is a reason why the guru in the cave has white hair and a beard down to his knees. There's a reason why the powerful Witch at the end of the forest has old, craggy skin and balks at seeing or talking with anyone.

Time. These wise old people have taken the time to learn, incorporate, fail, and succeed with their magical skills and knowledge. In this age of instant gratification and false advertising that everyone can be an overnight success, we have lost the appreciation of the time and effort it takes to truly become proficient or successful.

It takes time to practice; try and try again until these paths make sense to you. Get comfortable doing spell work, crafting a mojo, doing rituals, or simply feeling comfortable in your skin as a magical, spiritual person.

It has been said that there is nothing new under the sun. Nothing we practice is new, although it may be new to us.

The rites and practices we have learned are of the ancient ways and mysteries, so there is no need to rush. They have been with us since the first priest or priestess swept the steps of their sacred temple.

So take your time. Try things out one at a time. See what fits and what doesn't. Keep what works and discard what doesn't. And when you really get comfortable with the knowledge, add your own twists and flavors, words and chants and make the magick your own. For truly that is where the great power lies, when the magick becomes *your magick*.

You Are a Divine Being

Magick is empowering. Magick is fun. Hoodoo is powerful, and Vodou is a divine sacred religion.

Mojos bring comfort and a sense of well-being. Candles light up an altar and the dark places in our soul.

Salts, herbs, oils, and Florida Water help us cast spells. They aid us in our rites, rituals, and practices.

Graveyards soothe our worries and listen to our woes. Benevolent spirits lend a hand when called upon with proper respect and admiration.

Moving our bodies strengthens us and keeps us grounded and centered on the earth.

All the above are available to us to keep the good juju flowing through our daily lives, as we know life isn't always a bed of roses. There are good days, bad days, and some damned hard days in between.

And yet with all we've learned it comes down to one simple message:

YOU ARE A DIVINE BEING!

From the stars and across the sands of time you came, a soul, breathing and entering into the manifestation of life. You are blessed with an inner knowledge and guidance, should you choose to develop it, that will always be your core of truth and spiritual power.

You could choose to do nothing more than greet the dawn in the morning and say hello to the stars at night. And that would be enough, especially if you did it on a consistent, daily basis.

But I have assumed you need a bit more than that or you wouldn't have picked up this book. Some of us are drawn, pulled by forces we may not understand, to the Divine Mysteries and the occult. We feel at home with candles, oils, and spells. We enjoy helping others and ourselves with our spiritual knowledge and gifts, and we feel ecstatic bliss when we join with others of like mind.

As you journey along this path, you may encounter others who do not share your beliefs, works, or visions. That's okay! Let them be. Know the divinity within yourself that brought you here is true for you. Proceed as you see fit with what works for you.

It has been a pleasure and an honor to be here with you. From my deepest heart of hearts, I thank YOU for reading this book and taking the time to be with me.

May all your works be successful ones!

lagniappe

THIS BOOK HAS BEEN an outpouring of my heart and soul. Please know I deeply appreciate your readership!

As a thank you that is customary in the fabulous city of New Orleans, I offer you a lagniappe in closing. *Lagniappe* is a Creole word that means *gift* or *treat*, somewhat akin to a baker's dozen (getting thirteen doughnuts for twelve) or a little juicy goodness that falls off your po-boy sandwich onto your plate, or some yummy extra sauce or gravy. I hope these extra goodies will aid you on your continued journey as a magical, mystical, spiritual person!

Suggested Books

The following books have had a tremendous effect on my life, enhancing my knowledge and thirst to carry on as a person who practices magick, and believes in the spirit and power of the universe. The list below includes nonfiction and fiction titles:

Andrews, Ted. *Animal-Speak: The Spiritual and Magical Powers of Creatures Great and Small*. St. Paul, MN: Llewellyn Worldwide Publishing, 1998.

This was a pioneer book in introducing information on how to work with animal totems and guides. It is phenomenal in its ability to be a reference guide for spiritual and metaphysical meanings behind the encounters we have with the animal world in our daily lives and is a must-have book for any person on the magical path.

DeGrasse Tyson, Neil. *Astrophysics for People in a Hurry*. New York: W.W. Norton and Company, 2015.

This book helps us to ground into the world of science and expand our knowledge of the cosmos. One always needs to be looking up, making contact with our sky and stars on a daily basis. Many early scientists were once exiled or spurned for their beliefs about the cosmos. As people on the magical path, science balances our practices in the world of folk magick, the occult, and the Craft. Knowledge is power, and it is good to know basic information about our universe.

Farrar, Janet, and Stewart Farrar. *A Witches' Bible*. Blaine, WA: Phoenix Publishing, Inc., 1981.

This book is the quintessential encyclopedia of Witchcraft, history, and lore and belongs on the shelf of any person seeking or dedicated to the Craft. It is filled with rituals, amazing photos, and information to which one can return to again and again, as they grow in knowledge and magical power.

Horsley, Kate. *Confessions of a Pagan Nun*. Boston, MA: Shambala Publications, 2001.

    This is a work of fiction that will rip your heart and spur your soul. It carries you into the life of a woman living during a critical time in history when Druidic beliefs and practices were being condemned and replaced by the power and beliefs of the Christian Church.

Orwell, George. *Nineteen Eighty-Four.* New York, NY: Harcourt Brace Jovanovich, 1949.

    This is a chilling work of fiction, written more than seventy years ago, yet it could have been written today. Its story and protagonist closely mirror today's world of language and things that are false appearing real. Many people read this book during their high school English classes, but in today's political climate it deserves a second read.

Sams, Jamie, and David Carson. *Medicine Cards.* New York: St. Martin's Press, 1988.

    The oracle cards and book provide a unique and insightful opportunity to work with animals as a tool of divination. The cards are beautifully illustrated, and the text takes the reader's mind into the spirit world of animals, and how they can assist one on their spiritual path.

Smith, Ronald. *Hoodoo.* New York: Clarion Books, 2015.

    This work of fiction tells the story of a young African-American boy who must solve a mystery by connecting with his ancestors, practicing Hoodoo and Conjure. Set in a small town in Alabama, *Hoodoo* grabs your imagination and takes you into the world of African-American folk magick, practiced as a sacred art and beloved history passed down from generation to generation.

Starhawk. *The Fifth Sacred Thing.* New York: Bantam Books, 1993.
This work of fiction opened the doors of belief to what living in magical intention and in a sacred community might look like. It was a forerunner of its time, grabbing the hearts of those who longed to live in communities where magical practices and structure were of the norm and not relegated as "hippy-dippy," or "alternative." Although a work of fiction, many practices, circles, and festivals owe a debt of gratitude to Starhawk for her incredible vision and ability to paint the picture of how the community of Earth might thrive and survive if only magick was the river to which we all came to for sustenance and sustainability.

Magick Tips

Here are a few tips I've learned along the way as a practitioner of magick:

- A pushpin works great for poking holes in candles.
- Less is more. Use restraint when adding oils to candles. Too much oil can cause the wick not to burn.
- A burning stick of incense works fabulously as a magick wand.
- Save your remnants (string, candle wax, clippings, papers, ashes) from your spell workings. Place them in a bucket. When the bucket is full, bury the remnants in your back-

yard or if you live where you don't have a yard, bury them in a container filled with dirt. That way, the magick is always with you.

- If you have magical statues or paintings in your home, be sure to bless them on a regular basis.

- Put protective herbs, blessed salt, or red brick dust under your front door mat, for protection.

- When you first see the moon on any given day, blow it a kiss of acknowledgment.

- If you put out decorations on Halloween, say a prayer over them, bless them, and anoint them with your favorite Witchy oil.

- If a mojo becomes tattered and torn after years of working, enclose the old mojo inside a new mojo, to keep the power strong and pass the good juju from the old mojo to the new mojo.

- If you frequent thrift or secondhand clothing stores, always smudge your items before you wear them, or set them out in your home. This is an acknowledgment to the previous owner and clears any energy attached to the item before you claim it as your own.

- Battery-operated candles are fabulous stand-ins for traditional candles. You can take them anywhere and use them anywhere, without worrying about fire danger or smoke. Look for battery-operated candles in craft stores, home furnishing stores, and hardware stores.

Suggested Movies

I love movies. Here's a list of some of my magical favorites:

Eve's Bayou (1997) written and directed by Kasi Lemmons, an African-American woman, who made her directorial debut with this movie

Stars: Samuel L. Jackson, Lynn Whitfield, Jurnee Smollet-Bell, Meagan Good, Debi Morgan

This was one the first films that took viewers into the realm of African-Americans and Hoodoo in a way that drew in viewers and made them want to saunter down long, hot roads covered with the shady branches of ancient live oak trees from whose branches swing tendrils of Spanish moss. It also features a mostly African-American cast, which is a treat in to-day's world of homogenized films.

Interview with the Vampire (1994) screenplay by Anne Rice, directed by Neil Jordan.

Stars: Tom Cruise, Brad Pitt, Antonio Banderas, and Kirsten Dunst

This movie brings the old city of mysterious New Orleans and its cast of the vampires, statues, and cemeteries onto the screen in ways that make magick seem possible. It's a trip into the world of the not so distant past, combined with imagery that makes your imagination take flight into the lands of what could be possible, if one is willing to believe.

Practical Magic (1998) based on the novel by Alice Hoffman, screenplay by Robin Swicord, directed by Griffin Dune

    Stars: Sandra Bullock, Nicole Kidman, Stockard Channing, and Dianne Wiest

    This movie is for the everyday Witch and any woman who knows the power of making wishes. It features believable acts of Witchcraft such as casting a circle, using a spell book, and other fantastical acts all set in a quaint little town beside the sea that anyone would love to call home. Its cast of magical aunts, beautiful scenery, and women who discover they are truly powerful make this trip into the world of the Craft a memorable one.

Poltergeist (1982) directed by Tobe Hooper, screenplay by Steven Spielberg

    Stars: JoBeth Williams, Heather O'Rourke, Craig T. Nelson

    This original version is scary, thrilling, and makes you believe there are spirits around us every day, some good and some not so good. It shows the strength of a woman who will go to any lengths to protect her children and the power of mediumship; it also has a creepy real-life urban legend to go along with the disturbing premise. A must-have, must-see movie for anyone who believes in ghosts.

The Fifth Element (1997) written and directed by Luc Besson

    Stars: Bruce Willis, Milla Jovovich, Gary Oldman, Chris Tucker

    This movie is sci-fi, action, and adventure at its best. It takes us into a relatable future in which only the fifth element can save us from destruction. Several lines from the film speak to us as magical people, who honor the elements and their power.

The Skeleton Key (2005) directed by Iain Softley, written by Ehren Kruger

Stars: Kate Hudson, Peter Sarsgaard, Joy Bryant

This movie is creepy and intense, filled with haunting images and a story line that will make you believe in the power of red brick dust, Hoodoo, and Conjure. It features the wonderful countryside of Louisiana as well as some brief stops in the Crescent City of New Orleans. It shows magick lives right alongside us in our everyday lives, whether one chooses to believe in it, or not.

BiBLiOGraphy

Books

Benjamin, Michael. *The Lesser Banishing Ritual of the Pentagram: A 21st Century Grimoire.* Stafford, England: Megalithica Books, 2014.

Bethards, Betty. *The Dream Book: Symbols for Self-Understanding.* Boston, MA: Element Books, Inc. 1977.

Bivins, N.D.P. *Original Black & White Magic by Marie Laveau.* International Imports, 1991.

Cunningham, Scott. *Cunningham's Encyclopedia of Magical Herbs.* St. Paul, MN: Llewellyn Publications, 1998.

Davidson, Gustav. *A Dictionary of Angels.* New York: The Free Press, 1967.

Fitch, Ed. *A Grimoire of Shadows.* St. Paul, MN: Llewellyn Publications, 1997.

Glassman, Sallie Ann. *Vodou Visions.* New York: Villard Books, 2000.

Lowenthal, Wolfe. *There Are No Secrets.* Berkeley, CA: Blue Snake Books, 1991.

Martinié, Louis, and Sallie Ann Glassman. *The New Orleans Voodoo Tarot.* Rochester, Vermont: Destiny Books, 1992.

Sed, Herb. *J.M. Nickell's Botanical Ready Reference.* Beaumont, CA: Trinity Center Press, 1976.

Saxon, Lyle. *Fabulous New Orleans.* New York: The Century Company, 1928.

Teish, Luisah. *Jambalaya.* New York, NY: Harper and Row, 1988.

Witches Almanac. *The Witches' Almanac Spring 2015–2016.* Providence, RI: The Witches' Almanac, 2014.

Yronwode, Catherine. *Hoodoo Herb and Root Magic.* Forestville, CA: The Lucky Mojo Curio Company, 2002.

Websites

The Seven-Day Week and the Meanings of the Names of the Day.
http://www.crowl.org/Lawrence/time/days.html#

African Drum Music
http://www.music-mosaic.com/articles/african-drum-music.htm

Haitian Drum Music
https://steampunkopera.wordpress.com/2011/07/19/haitian-drumming-for-dummies/
http://www.bongamusic.org/hdrums.php

Drums of India
http://www.chandiramani.com/drumsofindia1.html

Native American Drums
http://sun.sunreed.com/NativeAmericanDrums.htm

Palo Santo

   https://sacredwoodessence.com/benefits/

The Angel Oak

   https://www.atlasobscura.com/places/the-angel-oak-tree

Western Syncretic Religion and Countries

   https://www.howard.edu/library/reference/cybercamps/
camp2002/YorubaFaith.htm

Florida Water

   https://shaheenmiroinsights.com/the-gypsys-tricks-for
-spiritual-cleansing-and-protection-florida-water/

   http://www.nydailynews.com/making-splash-old
-fashioned-florida-water-cures-ails-ya-smells-good
-article-1.828293#

Journal Article

Grant, Richard. "The Whispering of the Trees." *Smithsonian*
(Washington, DC) 48, no. 10 (March 2018).